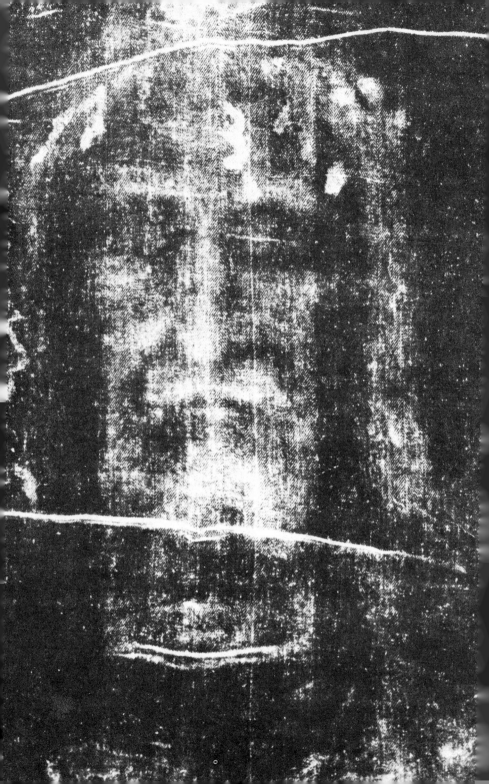

THE TESTIMONY
OF THE SHROUD

Deductions from the photographic and written
evidence of the Crucifixion and Resurrection of
Jesus Christ

RODNEY HOARE

St. Martin's Press
New York

Library of Congress Cataloging in Publication Data

Hoare, Rodney.
    Testimony of the Shroud.

    Bibliography: p.
    Includes index.
    1. Holy Shroud—Controversial literature. I.   Title.
BT587.S4H59   232.9'66   78-4385
ISBN 0-312-79354-5

Quotations from the New English Bible, second edition,
© 1970, by kind permission of the Oxford and
Cambridge University Presses.

CONTENTS

BLACK AND WHITE PLATES

ACKNOWLEDGEMENTS

A book such as this one is really a combined effort, and when I mention a few by name, it must be remembered that there were many others. Selection is difficult, but I think it is true to say that of all the forensic scientists I consulted, Mr Lee was the most outstandingly helpful; that I obtained much of the medical information from Dr Bill Watson of Shrewsbury; and that my main theological source was the Rev. Robin Protheroe, with whom I have enjoyed many discussions on the subject. I have had a lot of encouragement from friends, especially from Vernon Armitage, and Colonel Cyril Jarvis, under whom I served in the 1st Gurkha Rifles.

The most valuable support has been from my wife and three children. A commanding interest of this sort can be the ruin of relationships, but for years my family has accepted my frequent disappearances into the study, the thumping of my typewriter, and the monotony of hearing me discuss the subject with others, with patience and cheerfulness.

My thanks to them all.

INTRODUCTION

Jesus Christ.

His name is spoken by millions, in tones varying from worship and faith to disbelief and mindless oath. He is still, to many, the greatest man ever to have lived. The religion he founded has more nominal adherents than any other, and has changed the lives of some so that they have achieved astonishing deeds for the benefit of man; others have used the name of Christ to justify wars, even against fellow-Christians of different creeds.

Just think what his influence has been on history, and is in the world today. And then remember that he was born, illegitimate, into a carpenter's family, in an obscure province in the Roman Empire. Some of his words and actions from the last two years of his life are recorded – very wise teaching and some remarkable deeds – but he plainly had little effect on the authorities, and was regarded by them as a rebel and charlatan.

What is recorded of his life does not explain the tremendous effect he has had. Many other personalities through the centuries have left words of profound wisdom, and some have been credited with remarkable cures, but they have barely rippled the surface of the flow of life, whereas Jesus turned the tide.

The key lies at his life's end. The authorities put him to death by a criminal's death, and his closest followers were scattered. Memories of him should have lingered on for only a short time, barely beyond the deaths of those who had known him well. But, and what a but! he is reported to have come to life again, changing his lost, unimpressive and provincial band of followers into the bold cornerstones of the future church. It was the Resurrection that made Christianity, as St Paul pointed out (1 Corinthians 15: 14).

But did the Resurrection *really* take place? Can we believe it today?

For many the very existence of the Church is the only evidence needed. For a great number, the Gospels are stamped with the hallmarks of truth, and the convincing honesty and trustworthiness of the other sections infect the description of the Resurrection with a similar credibility. Yet for a considerable proportion of people, the whole concept of the Resurrection is so alien to normal physical experience that they cannot accept it, and so a whole-hearted allegiance to Christianity is not possible. Disbelief in this feature of the story can spread to distrust of the whole, and it can even go far enough in some people for them to question whether there ever was such a historical person as Jesus.

The three days which began with the Crucifixion mark one of the most important turning points in history. What evidence is there to suggest what happened then? Is the evidence trustworthy? Can we learn anything new by re-examining it, applying the methods of modern analysis and detection?

1 THE WRITTEN EVIDENCE

We know a great deal about the times in which Jesus lived, and we would expect to find much information about him and his activities in contemporary writings. In fact, these sources are disappointing. Many of the incidental people mentioned in the Gospels – Pontius Pilate, Herod, Annas, Caiaphas and John the Baptist, for instance – are recorded in other historical sources, but there are some surprising gaps and silences about Jesus.

Surviving official records of the Roman administration do not mention him at all. Not until the activities of the Christians start entering the reports in the second century, does the life of Jesus make any impact on them. When we turn to contemporary Jewish historians, we fare little better. Philo of Alexandria, born twenty years before Jesus and dying twenty years after, does not name him once. Even more surprising, there was no word of him in the chronicle of Justus of Tiberias in Galilee, who was born about the time when Jesus died and must surely have been aware of the effect Jesus had had in his locality.

The most promising source would be Josephus, an able and extensive Jewish historian. Self-opinionated and well-born, he spent some years in Rome. When the Roman war against the Jews began in A.D. 66, he started by fighting for his countrymen, but then crossed over to join the conquerors.

His book *The Jewish War* came out in about A.D. 77, and his *Antiquities of the Jews* in A.D. 93. Josephus must have known about

Jesus. He was probably in Jerusalem when St Paul caused an uproar there in A.D. 57. He was in Rome in 64 when Nero's persecutions of the Christians began. In Book 20 of the *Antiquities*, he mentions the trial and stoning of James, 'the brother of Jesus who was called Christ'. And there is another, much-quoted reference to Jesus, where, in Book 18, the following appears:

Now there was about this time Jesus, a wise man, if it be lawful to call him a man; for he was a doer of wonderful works, a teacher of such men as receive the truth with pleasure. He drew over to him many of the Jews, and many of the Gentiles. He was [the] Christ. And when Pilate, at the suggestion of the principal men among us, had condemned him to the cross, those that loved him at the first did not forsake him; for he appeared to them alive again the third day; as the divine prophets had foretold these and ten thousand other wonderful things concerning him. And the tribe of Christians, so named from him, are not extinct to this day.

At first sight it seems valuable evidence of the historicity of Jesus. But the truth is not so simple. It is most unlikely that this paragraph was actually written by Josephus. It does not fit into the section of the book happily, and the implied adherence of Josephus to Christianity is unconvincing. While the paragraph was in the text by the fourth century, since Eusebius knew of it, the early Fathers of the Church, including Origen, did not, and stated categorically that Josephus did not accept Jesus as the Messiah.

This is the problem with written evidence from this period. If we had the author's manuscript in each case, we could be far more confident, but the oldest copies we have of these works are often the results of several successive copyists' efforts. The originals were put down on papyrus, and not until the third century was parchment used so that manuscripts could be preserved for a long time. The passage in Josephus was most probably inserted by an ardent Christian who had the task of making a copy; at any rate, he evidently edited the original words of Josephus considerably.

Once we disregard this paragraph as a probable insertion, the 'silence of Josephus' becomes most surprising, and the reason for it has been the subject of much debate. It must be remembered what kind of man he was, the times he was living in, and the fact that he was writing for the Roman people. The omission must have been deliberate, and it may simply have been that he considered it unwise to embark on a narrative which must have included the Jewish hopes of a Messiah to relieve them from oppression.

The main, in fact almost the only, sources of our knowledge of the life of Jesus are therefore the books of the New Testament. Here, again, we do not possess the authors' original manuscripts. No fragments of the books earlier than the second century have been found. The earliest copy we possess of the complete New Testament is the *Codex Sinaiticus* in the British Museum, which dates from about A.D. 331, or nearly three centuries after some of the books were written. To keep this in perspective, on the other hand, we must remember that the earliest copies we have of the works of Demosthenes, Plato, Sophocles, Aristophanes, Euripides and Catullus were written between twelve and sixteen centuries after the originals.

Investigation into the authorship and dates of the Gospels has been thorough, but the questions have not been, nor are likely to be, finally answered. The arguments will continue, many books being written on the subject each year. It is not easy to make statements of current thought which would have universal agreement, but there are some points which few would argue with.

First, the four Gospels are actually anonymous, and their authorship uncertain. The dates at which they were written are also unknown, but it is virtually certain that none was written for at least two decades after the death of Christ. As for their titles, we know they were named as the Gospels 'According to' Matthew, Mark, Luke and John as early as the second century. The term 'According to . . .' did not imply complete authorship. It probably indicated that some special material is contained in each Gospel which originated with the person named. Then, again, few would deny that the order in which they were written is not necessarily that in which they are printed. There is a strong likelihood that Mark's Gospel was the earliest, and was then expanded and added to by the authors of Matthew and Luke. St John's Gospel was probably written last, and independently of the others. Lastly it is worth pointing out that the direct, apostolic contributions, in the Gospels of St Matthew and St John, may have been very small.

When we first encounter the Gospels when young, most of us picture them as having been set down by the evangelists named immediately after the events they describe. If only this were true! But as the illusions of first-hand authenticity are proved false, there is no necessity to swing to the other extreme, to 'demythologize' to the extent of denying any historical substance in the Gospels whatsoever.

There is little doubt that the Gospels set down the historical traditions of Jesus held by the early Church. They contain narrative accounts of Passion week, the Crucifixion and Resurrection, as well as remembered sequences of the teaching of Jesus. The times and places at which this teaching is said to have taken place may not necessarily be accurate, but the teaching itself has probably been remembered almost exactly. Prophets taught in verse to help their disciples to commit it to memory, and the recorded sayings of Jesus, their pattern and verse structure, if translated directly into Aramaic, suggest that the original words may have been passed on almost without alteration, particularly in view of the facility men then still had for absorbing and repeating very long spoken passages.

The extent to which one believes the Gospels to be historical truth depends on the reader. It depends also on how far he has researched into the subject. Some who have started out to delve into the historicity to strengthen their faith, have been disillusioned in the process. Others have retained their altered faith, like Schweitzer, for instance, who wrote in *The Quest for the Historical Jesus*:

We are experiencing what Paul experienced. In the very moment when we were coming nearer to the historical Jesus than men had ever come before, and were already stretching out our hands to draw Him into our own time, we have been obliged to give up the attempt and acknowledge our failure in that paradoxical saying: 'If we had known Christ after the flesh yet henceforth know we Him no more.' And further we must be prepared to find that the historical knowledge of the personality and life of Jesus will not be a help, but perhaps eveu an offence to religion . . .

Jesus as a concrete historical personality remains a stranger to our time, but His spirit which lies hidden in His words, is known in simplicity, and its influence is direct. Every saying contains in its own way the whole Jesus.

To the average committed Christian, whatever the critics may unearth, there is an emotional rather than a rational reason for accepting the Gospels. A sublime touch shines through the reported actions and words of Jesus beyond the capacity of human invention. Consequently it is possible to perceive, in all four Gospels, his unique character and inspired gifts. Our perceptions will not be uniform; nor does, for any one of us, every recorded word fit into the picture of Jesus we have formed. For example, my own conception of him convinces me that he has been misquoted in the sentence, 'No one comes to the Father except by me' (John 14: 6).

Likewise I cannot believe that he thought that all who came before him were thieves and robbers (John 10: 8), and there are several other sayings, and even actions, like the cursing of the fig-tree, which, though probably based on words witnessed by the apostles, must have been misinterpreted or misquoted before being set down – if my conception of Jesus is correct.

Yet others will have different conceptions, and these sayings may then allow interpretations which fit in with them. It would, after all, be difficult for any serious reader to believe that every word in the New Testament is the 'Gospel truth'. There are definite contradictions between the books which mean that all of them cannot be true. What was the actual wording of the notice on the Cross, for instance? Each of the four Gospels gives a different version. Which women went to the tomb, and what did they do there and find? And how can anyone believe that Judas died by hanging himself (Matthew 27: 5) as well as by falling forward on the ground and bursting open so that his entrails poured out, as Luke reports in Acts (1: 18)? It is a physical impossibility for both to have happened. The fact must be faced that, with regard to the times of events, the personalities and places involved, there are considerable inconsistencies between the various accounts, and not every detail can be categorically true.

This must be watched when we study the remarkably detailed accounts of the Crucifixion and Resurrection. They include some very specific observations, such as the flow of a mixture of blood and water from the wound, the time when each action took place, and the weight of spices left in the tomb. Also the words spoken by Jesus, the centurion, the thieves and passers-by are recorded. Can they all have been accurately remembered?

It is true that St John's Gospel may at this point reflect the eye-witness report of John himself, and St Mark's Gospel, and therefore St Matthew's and St Luke's, may be incorporating the memories of the apostle Peter. But none of these accounts was written down for at least twenty years, so that facts may well have become distorted over time and many repetitions. Therefore how much reliance can be placed on them?

What we need to confirm these stories is an independent record made at the actual time of the events and still preserved in its original form. Remarkably, and astoundingly, that is what we possess if the Holy Shroud of Turin is indeed genuine.

This forensic, almost photographic, image on a long strip of linen, is said to have been formed when the body of Jesus was taken down from the Cross and laid in the cloth. Scientists have demonstrated that it is no forgery, and Popes have testified to its authenticity. Yet the public is rarely allowed to see it – apart from a television programme, the exposition in September 1978 will be the first time it has been on open display since 1933 – and international scientists have been denied access to it by the Roman Catholic Church, its curators. What story is told by this remarkable pattern of stains which needs to be so well guarded? Christianity, after all, never ought to be afraid of the truth.

It is the aim of this book to examine the evidence provided by this 'Fifth Gospel', if that is what it is, with the aid of forensic scientists, doctors and others, and see what light it can throw on what we know of Christ's Crucifixion and Resurrection from the written evidence.

2 THE HISTORY OF THE SHROUD

To prove the authenticity of the Shroud from historical sources is out of the question. We would need to be able to state where it was and who had guarded it at every stage of its existence, and not even that would satisfy everyone. If the validity of the relic is to be proved it must be done in other ways – it must, in effect, be able to provide its own verification. An examination of the known history of the Shroud is nevertheless important.

First, let us look at the Gospel accounts which refer to Christ's burial:

> When evening fell, there came a man of Arimathea, Joseph by name, who was a man of means, and had himself become a disciple of Jesus. He approached Pilate, and asked for the body of Jesus; and Pilate gave orders that he should have it. Joseph took the body, wrapped it in a clean linen sheet, and laid it in his own unused tomb, which he had cut out of the rock; he then rolled a large stone against the entrance, and went away. Mary of Magdala was there, and the other Mary, sitting opposite the grave. [Matthew 27: 57–61]

> By this time evening had come; and as it was Preparation-day (that is, the day before the Sabbath), Joseph of Arimathea, a respected member of the Council, a man who was eagerly awaiting the kingdom of God, bravely went in to Pilate and

asked for the body of Jesus. Pilate was surprised to hear that he was already dead; so he sent for the centurion and asked him whether it was long since he died. And when he heard the centurion's report, he gave Joseph leave to take the dead body. So Joseph bought a linen sheet, took him down from the cross, and wrapped him in the sheet. Then he laid him in a tomb cut out of the rock, and rolled a stone against the entrance. And Mary of Magdala and Mary the mother of Joseph were watching and saw where he was laid. [Mark 15: 42-7]

Now there was a man called Joseph, a member of the Council, a good, upright man, who had dissented from their policy and the action they had taken. He came from the Jewish town of Arimathea, and he was one who looked forward to the Kingdom of God. This man now approached Pilate and asked for the body of Jesus. Taking it down from the cross, he wrapped it in a linen sheet, and laid it in a tomb cut out of the rock, in which no one had been laid before. It was Friday, and the Sabbath was about to begin.

The women who had accompanied him from Galilee followed; they took note of the tomb and observed how his body was laid. [Luke 23: 50-55]

The three accounts are remarkably similar, and it is quite clear in each that a shroud was needed for a rapid, temporary burial. The women see the way the body is interred and where. But when we turn to the account in St John's Gospel, we have quite a different story:

After that, Pilate was approached by Joseph of Arimathea, a disciple of Jesus, but a secret disciple for fear of the Jews, who asked to be allowed to remove the body of Jesus. Pilate gave the permission; so Joseph came and took the body away. He was joined by Nicodemus (the man who had first visited Jesus by night), who brought with him a mixture of myrrh and aloes, more than half a hundredweight. They took the body of Jesus and wrapped it, with the spices, in strips of linen cloth according to Jewish burial-customs. Now at the place where he had been crucified there was a garden, and in the garden a new tomb, not yet used for burial. There, because the tomb was near at hand and it was the eve of the Jewish Sabbath, they laid Jesus. [John 19: 38–42]

What a contradiction here! Although they had to leave the body in a near-by tomb because it was almost sundown and the start of the Sabbath, they did have time to wash and anoint the body and wrap it in strips as was the proper custom. Plainly no shroud was therefore used.

Who are we to believe? It is not fair to count it as three against one when the three may be a single source. Matthew, Mark and Luke are called the Synoptic Gospels as their narratives are generally from the same points of view, and in this case one eyewitness may have described the event to Mark, who was largely copied by Matthew and Luke. In that case, there is an interesting omission from the two reproductions – the purchase by Joseph of the linen – and some equally interesting additions. But, basically, it is reduced to a straight disagreement between the Synoptics and John, and many people consider that John wins when his next section is taken into account.

Early on the Sunday morning, while it was still dark, Mary of Magdala came to the tomb. She saw that the stone had been moved away from the entrance, and ran to Simon Peter and the other disciple, the one whom Jesus loved. 'They have taken the Lord out of his tomb,' she cried, 'and we do not know where they have laid him.' So Peter and the other set out and made their way to the tomb. They were running side by side, but the other disciple outran Peter and reached the tomb first. He peered in and saw the linen wrappings lying there, but did not enter. Then Simon Peter came up, following him, and he went into the tomb. He saw the linen wrappings lying, and the napkin which had been over his head, not lying with the wrappings but rolled together in a place by itself. Then the disciple who had reached the tomb first went in too, and he saw and believed; until then they had not understood the scriptures, which showed that he must rise from the dead. [John 20: 1–9]

Now plainly this sounds like an eyewitness account rather than a record of the tradition handed down. St John tells us what he actually saw, and we feel we must believe him. He then seems to draw the conclusion from the positions of the wrappings that the body had been prepared for burial properly, and that it had disappeared supernaturally, leaving the bonds to fall from the positions they had occupied round it.

If we accept this, no shroud can have been used. The relic in Turin is in this case a forgery and the Synoptic Gospels wrong.

This section in St John has for years been the main argument in the attack on the authenticity of the Shroud, and a very powerful argument it is. Nevertheless, as will be shown later, the marks on the Shroud itself provide strong evidence for John's Gospel being absolutely accurate in its description of what John and Peter found in the tomb, but also for their interpretation of what they saw having been wrong. The Synoptics are in this case just as correct, as we shall see.

Thus there is, right at the beginning of the story, suspicion and doubt. Even if these initial uncertainties could be resolved, the next ones in the relic's history may never be.

Up to the fourteenth century, the whereabouts of the Shroud cannot be traced with certainty, except occasionally. References which may apply to it occur vaguely and intermittently, appearing like well-spaced street-lights on a very foggy night. One or two of the references seem fairly specific, like the one describing how a French bishop, Arculf, saw it being openly venerated in Jerusalem in A.D. 670, and they become clearer as time goes by, until there can be little doubt it was in Constantinople in about the year A.D. 1,000 and was brought to France from there, perhaps, by a returning Crusader, in about the thirteenth century.

There may well be more to learn about the first thousand years of its existence. A convincing case has been made in an article by Ian Wilson (*Catholic Herald*, 16 November 1973) for the Shroud being identical with the relic known as the Holy Mandylion. This is reputed to have been a miraculous piece of linen which showed the face of Jesus only, brought to Edessa (Urfa) in Turkey. Among others whom it converted was King Abgar (A.D. 13–50), who was contemporary with Jesus. It is suggested that this was, in fact, the Turin Shroud folded to show the face only, and if this is so the whereabouts of the Shroud can be traced for the greater part of its existence, for in 944 the Mandylion was brought from Edessa to Constantinople, when reports of the Shroud being there begin, and only disappeared without trace in 1204 when the Crusaders captured the city.

Soon after that the Shroud surfaced in France, and its story then becomes more certain. Quite a number of its movements are known, together with its owners, and in 1452 it was passed to the royal house of Savoy, which has owned it ever since.

On 4 December 1532, when it was at Chambèry in France, it was very nearly destroyed. There was a disastrous fire in the sacristy of Sainte-Chappelle, where it was kept in a silver casket. Four men dragged it out from the blazing inferno. Drops of molten metal fell on the cloth, burning through the folds, and though it was carefully repaired by nuns, the burns, scorchmarks and patches left vivid patterns the length of the cloth. On photographs, the darker parts are portions of the cloth that were burnt and carbonized, while the white triangles are patches replacing the parts destroyed. The square patches seen at the centre and at the sides are portions of the cloth not touched by the water used to extinguish the fire. Luckily it is between the worst patches and lines that the vital stains in the form of the front and back of a body can be seen.

In 1578, four centuries ago, the Shroud was moved to Turin, and since 1664 it has been in the special shrine built for it overlooking the high altar in the cathedral.

Plainly there are many gaps and uncertainties in the story, and we cannot accept the Shroud purely on historical grounds. One would hardly expect a watertight case for a relic of such antiquity anyway. The Christians who valued it were persecuted and driven underground on many occasions in the first few centuries, and the whole Palestinian area was often á battleground, Jerusalem and other cities being completely destroyed on more than one occasion. In the circumstances, a stable and well-authenticated preservation of any relic was far more than could be expected, and the chance of such an object surviving seems so improbable that any such claim must be examined extremely critically.

What we do know for certain in the case of the Shroud is that it has remained unchanged in Turin for four centuries. A sixteenth-century painting shows that the pattern of stains was on it then. Beyond that, the Shroud has to provide its own proof.

Plate **1** Above: Turin, home of the Shroud, a large industrial town in north-west Italy, close to the Alps

Plate **2** Below: The larger dome (with spire) covers the Royal Chapel where the Shroud is kept. It was built in 1694 behind the high altar of the fifteenth-century cathedral

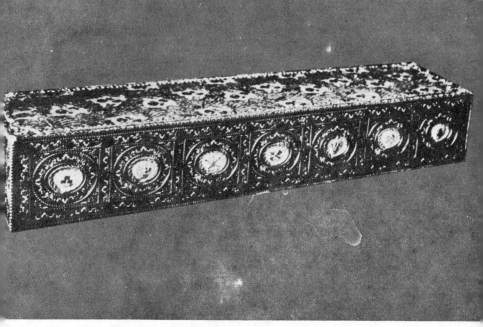

Plate 3 Above: The silver chest which contains the Shroud, wound on a roller and backed by red silk

Plate 4 Below: The chest is kept above the altar behind two iron grilles

3 THE HOLY SHROUD OF TURIN

The Shroud is a large sheet, 14 feet 4 inches long and 3 feet 7 inches wide, made of a mixture of cotton and linen. It is woven in a herringbone pattern, and is said to be identical in material and weave to many fabrics from the Near East of between the

Plate 5 The Holy Shroud

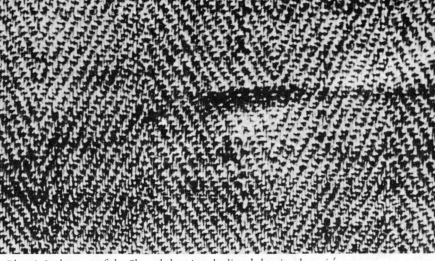

Plate 6 A close-up of the Shroud showing the linen's herring-bone
pattern

first and third centuries. There is no doubt that it could have been
made at the time of Christ, but its type is not exclusive to that
exact period, nor to Palestinian manufacture. A piece of cloth of
exactly the same weave has recently been discovered and in-
disputably dated A.D. 130–31.

A common reaction is to ask how it is possible for a material
to have survived for nearly two thousand years. But what actions
destroy materials? They are usually worn out, and then discarded with other refuse for burning or burial; or else they are
eaten by moths. A sacred object from the outset, the Shroud
would always have had very careful handling, and would not
have been significantly reduced by abrasion. Also it would have
been kept in a casket or mothproof container for most of the time.
Only an unfortunate accident could have destroyed it. Plenty of
other pieces of material have survived as long or longer. There
are examples in the British Museum, for instance, or in the
Louvre or the Egyptian Museum at Turin.

To judge the Shroud's age by the weave and material is one
test, but there are alternative methods of confirmation, and for

some years there have been calls for it to be dated by the Carbon 14 method. The plants from which the material was originally made absorbed a certain, known proportion of this radioactive isotope while still alive, and since it disintegrates at a progressive known rate, the proportion of Carbon 14 which remains can give the age of the fabric. So far all requests for such a test have been refused, and it is true that, to carry it out, a small amount of the material would have to be burnt, and that even then the margin of error covers a considerable number of years. But the techniques are improving, and Dr Walter McCrone, a microanalyst from Chicago, considers that no more than a 4-millimetre square would be required with a new method using a mass spectrometer. Instead of measuring the disintegration rate of the Carbon 14, which is a slow process, it measures the proportion of the remaining Carbon 14 to the stable Carbon 12 atoms in the material. In this way all the Carbon 14 atoms in the material take part in the measurement instead of just those that disintegrate in a set time, and so far less material is needed. With a piece weighing no more than 1 milligram, an estimate of the age of the material should be possible within an accuracy of 50 years in 2,000. Nor would the Shroud need to be freshly cut, for two pieces of the material, one weighing 110 and the other 55 milligrams, which were removed from it some time ago, could provide samples for measurement once permission is given.

A quite different method of establishing the age of the cloth has already been used by Dr Max Frei, a criminologist who is the retired head of the Police Scientific Laboratory in Zürich. His exciting technique also charts any areas in which the Shroud has been exhibited, for Dr Frei is an expert in pollen analysis. Every species of flowering plant produces pollen grains – the male cells which are liberated to fertilize the female ones – and as unfortunate sufferers from hay fever will know, they penetrate nearly everywhere. The pollen grains of each species are characteristic, and can be distinguished by such details as size, shape, skin surface, protuberances and so on. Also they are almost indestructible, surviving for centuries in all sorts of environments, hot and cold, wet and dry. The uses of pollen analysis in forensic science are considerable, for the dust on an article or in the clothes of a criminal can show where it or he have been travelling. This is because, as the vegetation alters with area or season, so does the pollen. Also, because plants may change in an area over the course of centuries as mutations alter them, pollen can be used to date archaeological evidence where the pollen from extinct plants is present. It is a new science, and a most promising one.

The way Dr Frei worked on the Shroud was as follows. He was allowed to remove dust from the borders of the linen by using adhesive tape. Examining it under a stereoscopic microscope at a magnification of 50 diameters, he separated out all the particles which looked like fibres, hairs from plants, spores or pollen grains. These were then studied at magnifications of up to 1,300 diameters.

Textbooks giving details of pollen found in different climates have yet to be written, so new is the subject, so Dr Frei had to make many journeys round Europe and Asia Minor in different seasons of the year, collecting examples of pollen for comparison. Nor are present-day examples the only ones that can be used, as the alluvia in the Jordan Valley and sediments from the bottoms of lakes provide, as microfossils, pollen from plants long extinct, and these can also be used for dating.

Dr Frei's work is not yet complete, but already he can say with certainty, from the number of pollen types found only in Palestine and its surrounding deserts, and from Anatolia in Turkey. that the Shroud has in its life been exhibited in those two areas as well as in Western Europe. The Anatolian pollen supports, in his opinion, the claim that the Shroud was exhibited in Edessa as the Mandylion when it left Palestine. Also, from the presence of pollen of that age, his tests confirm that the cloth is about two thousand years old. The possibility that the Shroud was forged in Western Europe at a much later date may therefore be discarded.

Now we must consider the marks on the material. These, as can be seen in the photographs, take the form of symmetrical patterns of scorch marks from the fire at Chambèry, with, between them, the faint imprints of a man's naked body, front and back, the tops of the images being towards the centre (see Plate 5). Ian Wilson has described it thus in his article:

The first impression was the colouring, which I knew only

from eyewitness accounts of previous showings. The cloth itself had the colour of old ivory, but the images of Christ's body, and the burn-marks from a fire which had nearly destroyed the cloth in 1532, were a complete study in sepia – just like an early photograph.

Only when relatively close did one become aware of the quite separate colour of the bloodstains, a quite clear carmine-mauve, surprisingly vivid under the powerful television lights, much less distinct when they were switched off.

Subsequently I was able to examine the Shroud on no less than five separate occasions, for hours at a time, including studying both body and bloodstains under a powerful magnifying glass. Allowed such proximity, the impulse was irresistible to touch the cloth, which along with others I did, reverently if somewhat surreptitiously, for it was officially disapproved.

The fabric was surprisingly soft in texture – somewhat like damask to touch, yet in weight light, and incredibly flexible. From the fineness of the weave, it was easy to believe this was no pauper's winding sheet, but the purchase of the rich Joseph of Arimathea.

The linen, we have seen, is probably genuine, and no one would question that the scorch-marks were made by the fire at Chambèry. It is the body-stains that pose the problem, and the claim that they were made by the body of Christ seems so fantastic as to arouse almost derision when first encountered, or, at any rate, the most extreme scepticism. Relics are notoriously suspect. There are enough pieces of the True Cross extant, it is said, to make several crucifixes. Rinaldi points out that we have records of forty-two shrouds which have claimed authenticity. Why should that of Turin be any more authentic than the rest?

It was photography that singled it out, and it is worth explaining how this happened.

The year 1898 was the fiftieth anniversary of the Statuto, the constitution of Sardinia, which was later adapted to become the legal code of Italy, and celebrations were held throughout the kingdom, as it was then. Most cities of note arranged events, and the festivities in Turin included a display for eight days of the Shroud, its most sacred relic.

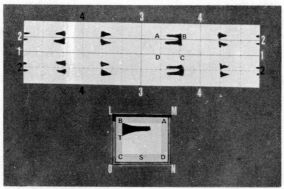

Plate 7 The stains caused by damage from the Chambery fire (1532) show how the Shroud was folded at that time. First it was folded lengthwise twice (1, 2), then across twice (3, 4), then crosswise twice again, but the last time the creases came a third of the way from each end. *Below:* the Shroud (ABCD) lay in the chest (LMNO). The side LM became the hottest – the black portion indicates the parts destroyed when molten metal dropped on one corner of the folded cloth. The triangle TCD shows the parts not affected by water when the fire was extinguished

About a million people came to see it, and during that time a keen amateur photographer, Secundo Pia, was allowed to expose two photographic plates to serve as an official record. He carefully took them back to his darkroom to process. He poured on the developer. Under the dim red safelight, an image slowly began to appear. As it intensified, Pia stared at it reverently. There was something uncanny about the image. The face and body, simply a pattern of stains on the Shroud, had revealed a roundness, a delicacy, a moulding on the photographic plate. There was a substantial, sublime quality about the image which made Secundo Pia feel he was indeed looking at the image of Jesus. The reality of the picture was so astonishing that he then made a contact print of it, so that it again appeared as on the Shroud. The quality had gone. Once more the stains looked lifeless and unimpressive.

Publication of the photographs caused a storm of controversy. It looked so extraordinary that people felt sure the negatives must be fakes. Yet official examination showed no evidence of forgery on the photographic plates. Two others who had photo-

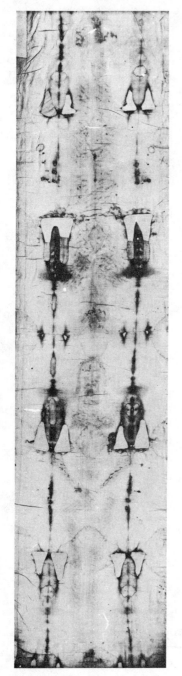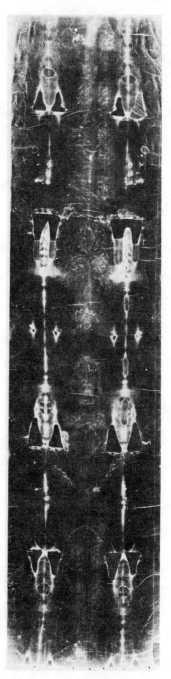

Plate 8 The Shroud as it appears on a positive and negative photograph

graphed the Shroud were found to have negatives which showed the same, impressively life-like images, though the prints from them turned out to be no more remarkable than the stains on the relic.

Here then was a strong argument against assertions that the images had been painted, probably by a fourteenth-century artist. Even granted that an artist may have tried to paint it in negative, for some reason, he could hardly have done so in a way that would have created a much more likely positive reversal. This assumption was reinforced when it was found that two well-known local artists, Reffo and Cussetti, had painted replicas of the Shroud during the exhibition, working directly from the original. In each case the copy looked just like the original, but, when photographed, the reversed images proved so distorted they could barely be recognized.

This, then, was how the image in the Turin Shroud demonstrated its claim to authenticity and the need for further research.

The main investigator over the next few years, at around the turn of the century, was a Frenchman, Paul Vignon. Born in 1865 of a wealthy Lyon family, Vignon was an outstanding mountaineer in his twenties, and his companion on some of his most difficult climbs had been a young Italian priest, Achille Ratti, later to become Pope Pius XI and an ardent supporter of the Shroud's authenticity. Vignon's other leading interests were biology and art, and he was himself an accomplished artist.

In 1900, one of France's most distinguished scientists, Yves Delages, who was a professor at the Sorbonne, showed Vignon Pia's photographs of the Shroud. He was at once impressed and disturbed by them, and determined to make the relic the subject of thorough investigation. Using special prints on glass which he obtained from Pia in Turin, he quickly came to the conclusion that no artist could have painted the image. Among his reasons he listed the following:

First, there were no signs of brushmarks or strokes on the surface. The shading was gradual, and whereas an artist's outlines and strokes are always visible under a microscope, none were detectable on the Shroud.

Secondly, the fabric was light, and could not have held pigment. Colouring matter applied by an artist years before would, in any

Plate 9 This painting by the sixteenth-century artist, Guilio Clovio, shows how the Shroud was folded over the body

case, have come off with frequent folding and unfolding. In fact it was the fibres which were stained, and the image went right through the cloth, though it was a shade lighter on the reverse side.

Thirdly, the negative image would have been impossible to paint, particularly before 1578. No artist then (or even now) would have had the skill, nor would he have had any reason to try and paint it other than in positive.

Fourthly, no early artist would have painted Christ naked. Indeed, we find Clovio's sixteenth-century painting of the Shroud altering it so as to show Christ in a loincloth.

These points seemed to show conclusively that the Shroud was not the work of a painter, but there are additional arguments to reinforce Vignon's findings, and the anatomical ones are particularly persuasive. In artistic works of the period in which the images could have been forged, figure painting was still primitive and unrealistic, the proportions wrong and anatomical details incorrect. Artists on the whole slavishly copied the conventions of artistic schools and older traditions. Yet the image on the Shroud is perfectly proportioned and anatomically correct down to the finest details, including the separation of the serum in the bloodstains. One most important point is the absence of thumbs in the images. It has been shown that the crucifixion nails would have damaged the median nerves in their penetration, pulling the thumbs across the palms. No artist in the Middle Ages could have known this; all would have shown the thumbs.

Vignon realized, however, that there were other ways of forging the images than by painting. A real body could have been used. He therefore coated a person's body with red chalk, and transferred the image to linen pressed on the surface. He tried the experiment several times, but the result was always blotchy, lifeless and unreal, whether reversed photographically or not. Later on similar experiments were conducted by Dr Judica and Dr Romanese, but in no case was the result at all satisfactory.

An even more remarkable demonstration that the image cannot have been forged has been carried out recently. Dr Eric Jumper and Dr John Jackson are assistant professors at the USAF Academy in Colorado. They obtained a photographic plate taken of the Shroud in 1931, and used a device called a microdensitometer to measure the relative densities of the image along the ridge line of the body. They then laid a sheet across the body of a friend who was similar in build to the body of the Shroud, and took accurate readings of the distance of the sheet from the skin along the ridge line. The correlation between image density and the distance of skin from material was remarkable.

To test this three-dimensional information in the Shroud, they used another device called an image analyser, and it converted the stain impressions into a recognizable, bas-relief type of image. For comparative purposes, they then tried other images, including photographic and painted portraits as well as direct contact images, and in no other instance did they obtain such a realistic effect. This is not really surprising, for both painter and camera record the tones seen, and these do not depend on distances in the third dimension. Even a copy of the Shroud, painted as accurately as possible by an artist, yielded a flat unrealistic result.

This three-dimensional evidence was in a remarkable way anticipated by Vignon. Having eliminated the possibility of forgery to his satisfaction, he presumed that there must have been a natural way for the stains to have developed in the linen when the dead body of a crucified person was laid in it. These had not, in his opinion, been produced simply by contact, however. They could only have acquired the gentle gradation of shading if they had been darkest where the linen had been resting on the skin's surface, decreasing in density as the distance from the skin became greater. This implied some sort of emanation from the skin which could act across a space – a gas probably – the effectiveness of which decreased the further away the cloth was from the body's surface. He therefore set out to find such an agent.

Trying to reproduce the probable formula for Jewish burial cloths, he soaked some linen in a mixture of myrrh and aloes with pure olive oil. By trial and error he eventually arrived at ammonia as giving stains of a similar colour to those in the Shroud. The next puzzle was to determine the circumstances in which a body could give off ammonia.

Most parents will know of one occasion in which this pungent gas is given off: when a baby's wet nappy is left for a while before being changed. In fact this example is highly relevant. The gas is given off because of the decomposition of urea in the baby's spent urine. Under rare circumstances, if a body is subjected to extreme pain – as in the prolonged agony of crucifixion – the body becomes covered with perspiration which contains a proportion of urea. Whoever the crucified man may have been, had his body been taken down from the cross and laid in the linen for at least twelve hours, the decomposition of the urea on the surface of his skin would have slowly emitted the ammonia to act on the aloes and stain the material. (A similar process occurs in the diazo method of making copies in reprography, ammonia also being the gas that stains the image in that case.) There is a limit to how long the process could have continued, for the body itself would have begun to decompose after about thirty-six hours, and this would have affected the cloth differently. The dead body must have been removed within that thirty-six-hour period, therefore, and this would apply however the images were made.

At this point it is valid to mention other theories which seek to explain the natural formation of stains by the crucified body. Some suggest different emanations. Many still favour a 'direct contact' theory: they believe that a constituent in the aloes reacted with the moisture from the body. At this stage we cannot settle which theory is correct, beyond saying that a natural cause for the staining is certainly possible, if not probable.

Having discounted the possibility of forgery, however, and shown that natural causes could explain it, there remains a third possibility, especially if the body was that of Jesus. It is probably true to say that by far the greatest number of people who believe in the authenticity of the Shroud would accept the supernatural explanation. There is in this case no need to discover, or even discuss, the method by which the stains were made, for with God all things are possible. A firm believer finds nothing incredible in the suggestion that God stepped outside the physical laws He made for the Universe to resurrect His Son, and in the process left the stains on the Shroud.

Some would qualify the supernatural explanation with natural elements, however, as in the 'Hiroshima' theory of Geoffrey Ashe, for instance. He reported in *Sindon*, a periodical which is entirely devoted to research into the Shroud, a test in which a brass ornament bearing the image of a horse in light relief was heated in a gas flame. It was then laid down with the relief upwards. A white handkerchief was placed on top, slightly stretched to prevent sagging. It received a scorch mark which bore a striking resemblance to the ornament, and a photographic negative of this gave a realistic positive picture. The scorch had been formed by direct contact and by radiation across a small space to give a realistic image containing varying tones. If the Resurrection was a momentary transformation by God of the mortal body to a glorified state, there could have been a supernatural release of energy at that instant which would have scorched the linen in the way we see it.

This last explanation presupposes that the body was that of Jesus, and we must next examine the evidence for such an assumption.

4 WHOSE WAS THE BODY?

What evidence is there in the Shroud that could help us to identify the person it contained? Let us study the photographs carefully.

To begin with, the stains show a perfectly proportioned man with a remarkably majestic face. His height should be easy to determine by measurement, but, perhaps because it depends on the directions in which the cloth was stressed, on how much to estimate the bend of the knees, on how high up one thinks the top of the head came, measurements have given values varying between 5 feet 4 inches and 6 feet 2 inches – a surprisingly wide variation.

We can see that the man was crucified. The Shroud clearly shows bloodstains from the nail-wounds in the upper wrist and the soles of the feet. This helps us to date and place the body. Crucifixion was probably first used by the Persians, and then spread to the Jews, Carthaginians and Romans. It was stopped altogether early in the fourth century by the Emperor Constantine, so the body was earlier than that. Since the Greeks and the Romans were clean-shaven, those nationalities may be eliminated. The shoulder-length hair and beard suggest a Jew, for as we know from depictions of Jewish prisoners-of-war between 37 B.C. and A.D. 70, they had unadorned hair and full beards. The body was probably that of a Jew, then, from some time in the first three centuries.

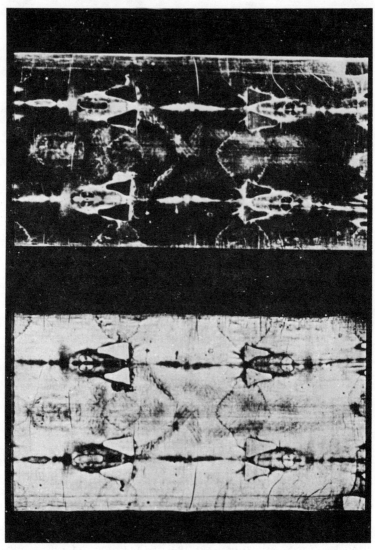

Plate 10 The image of the front of the body, positive and negative

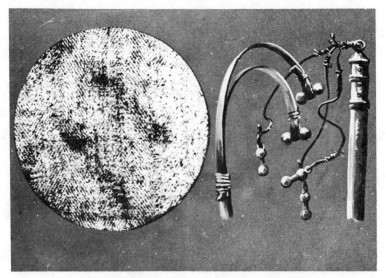

Plate 11 Close examination of the marks of the wounds show they were probably caused by scourging with a Roman flagrum – a lash with leather thongs weighted by a pair of joined balls of lead or a sheep's vertebra

There are visible on the body other signs of injury which might help in identification.

First, there was extensive bruising, as if the person had been buffeted around the face and body. Damage to the skin on the shoulder-blades suggests that he may have had to carry the heavy cross-beam of the cross for some way.

Secondly, there are marks over almost the entire body as if weals had been cut into the skin with whips. The lashes, perhaps 125 of them, are all over the back of the body down to the heels, and they tend to be in twos and threes, indicating scourging with a Roman flagrum by a man on each side. This was a whip with three thongs, each thong of which had a small piece of bone or metal tied to the end to bite into the flesh of the victim.

Thirdly, there are streaks of blood on the hair round the head, as well as on the forehead where a drip of blood trickled down and was deflected by the furrows into the shape of a figure '3'. These marks imply that he had to wear round his head something with sharp points digging into the skin.

Lastly, there is a large bloodstain on the right side, not far below the armpit, indicating a serious wound. From it, as can be seen on the back image, trickles of blood and water spread round the body when it was still horizontal, not long before being placed in the cloth.

Almost as significant are certain wounds which we would expect to be present but which are not. The legs, for instance, were not broken. It is almost impossible to imagine the degradation, agony and cruelty of a crucifixion. Nailed to the cross, the victim, if he allowed his body to sink so that his knees were bent and his weight was taken by his arms, found that his chest was fully expanded and he could not exhale. To breathe he therefore had to press up with his pierced feet, but this was at the price of an agonizing cramp in his muscles. This process, of going from one position to the other, could continue for a remarkably long time – some survived for three days at least – and the prisoner was usually put out of his agony by having his legs smashed, so that he could no longer press up to breathe.

Once dead, a body would then have been thrown into a communal grave, so the existence of the Shroud is an important clue in itself. No ordinary Jew would have been given a proper burial – crucifixion meant he was unclean and accursed of God – and even if he had been so exceptionally loved that friends came secretly to bury him in the proper fashion, they would have washed his body and anointed it, and then wrapped it up in strips of cloth before putting it in a tomb. There would have been no shroud in this case, either. Lacking any further information, it would be exceedingly difficult to think of an explanation for its existence.

This, then, is the visual evidence, and since it is claimed that the body was that of Jesus, we must examine it against the written evidence we have of him to see how they match.

At once the parallels become impressive. Christ was a Jew, of course, and he was crucified. We can consider the extensive bruising, and compare it with the Gospel accounts, Mark's, for instance: 'Some began to spit on him, blindfolded him, and struck him with their fists, crying out, "Prophesy!" And the High Priest's men set upon him with blows' (14: 15). Then the scourging: 'So Pilate, in his desire to satisfy the mob, released Barabbas to them; and he had Jesus flogged and handed him over to be crucified' (15: 25). It is a brief, harsh word, 'flogged', but horrifying to think of what it means. He would have been stripped, and his wrists tied to a low post little more than two feet high, so that he was unprotected from the cruel lashes of the flagellae of the soldier on each side. They would have given no mercy, those men. Victims sometimes died, their skins flayed from their backs.

Then there are the extraordinary bloodstains round the head, as if it had been spiked. 'Then the soldiers took him inside the courtyard [the Governor's headquarters] and called together the whole company. They dressed him in purple, and having plaited a crown of thorns, placed it on his head. Then they began to salute him with, "Hail, King of the Jews!" They beat him about the head with a cane and spat upon him, and then knelt and paid mock homage to him' (Mark 15: 16–19). A crown of thorns, followed by a beating about the head! Think what that implies. It certainly explains the bloodstains on the Shroud, and what are the chances of another man having been given a torture that could have left those same marks?

Already the agreement between the facts as we know them and the evidence of the Shroud is astonishing. Then there is the wound in the side; how did that occur? And why were the legs not broken?

Because it was the eve of the Passover, the Jews were anxious that the bodies should not remain on the cross for the coming Sabbath, since that Sabbath was a day of great solemnity; so they requested Pilate to have the legs broken and the bodies taken down. The soldiers accordingly came to the first of his fellow-victims and to the second, and broke their legs; but when they came to Jesus, they found that he was already dead, so they did not break his legs. But one of the soldiers stabbed his side with a lance, and at once there was a flow of blood and water. This is vouched for by an eyewitness, whose evidence is to be trusted. He knows that he speaks the truth, so that you too may believe. [John 19: 31–5]

Even the use of the Shroud is explained, as there was no time for the proper burial rites because they obtained Jesus's body only shortly before the Sabbath; and the surprisingly fine texture of the material used for wrapping up the crucified man's body is explained by the reported wealth of Joseph of Arimathea.

In all these points there is remarkable corroboration between the two sources of evidence, so that each seems to stand as guarantor of the other. Under Jewish law, a single witness had little value; at least two were required (Deuteronomy 17: 6 and 19: 15; Numbers 35: 30). On these grounds, in view of the agreement of two widely different types of evidence, the written and the photographic, the historicity of Jesus and his Crucifixion may be taken as proven.

Most appraisals of the Shroud have begun with an assumption of the complete accuracy of the Gospel accounts, and have tried to make the stains fit them. This has led to doubts of the Shroud's authenticity when certain stains, or the existence of the Shroud itself, have failed to match a particular description in a Gospel. However, the Shroud is material evidence that is available, and the marks on it can be seen, and prove themselves to have been formed on the day of the Crucifixion. It is therefore the Shroud which should stand as the measure of the accuracy of the Gospel stories, for there was plenty of opportunity for alteration and distortion in the decades before the traditions were first written down. The extent to which the Shroud confirms the accuracy of even small incidents reported in the Gospels means that more reliance can be placed on those details which the Shroud is unable to confirm.

So far as the Shroud is concerned, the evidence of the stains points with certainty towards their having been made by the body of Jesus. What else can we therefore learn from them?

5 FORENSIC EVIDENCE

Some of the most important research on the stains of the Shroud was done by Dr Pierre Barbet, a remarkable Paris surgeon. Born in 1883, he was an intensely religious man, and a linguist and violinist as well as a teacher of anatomy and a skilled surgeon.

His interest in the Shroud began in 1931. New, more detailed photographs than Pia's had just been taken by Giuseppe Enrie of Turin, and a friend of Barbet's asked him to make a short anatomical study of the figures in the stains. This simple introduction led to a detailed study which lasted many years, and the account of his research includes a most remarkable and moving account of the agonies Jesus must have suffered before and during the Crucifixion, on the evidence of the Shroud.

Apart from his natural gifts and experience and knowledge, he had available a supply of corpses to help him in his investigation. Among the most interesting experiments he conducted were those connected with the nail-wounds in the wrists as shown on the Shroud. Artists have always portrayed Jesus as having been crucified with nails driven through the palms of the hands, and saints who have borne stigmata have also had wounds on the palms, though admittedly this has mystical significance only. But Jesus is also recorded as having said to Thomas, 'Reach your finger here; see my hands' (John 20:27).

To investigate this, Barbet nailed through the palms of a dead

43

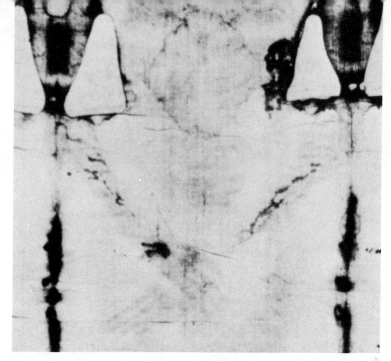

Plate 12 Above: Detail of wounds in the hands and side

body from his Paris hospital on to the cross-beam of a crucifix, and then raised it to the vertical. Immediately the weight of the body led the nails to tear through the flesh. Unless they had placed a further support rope round the arms and the bar of a wooden rest jutting out under the groin, the Roman executioners could not have nailed the palms in this way.

He then took an amputated arm, and tried to drive a nail through the wrist bones in the approximate position indicated by the bloodstains on the Shroud. To his surprise the nail forced its way through quite easily, and with the nail in this position the bone structure would have given enough purchase to prevent the nail from tearing its way free. This must have been the method the Romans used, and which had been forgotten soon after the practice of crucifixion was discontinued.

There was a remarkable bonus to the experiment, for it was at this point that Barbet found that the passage of the nail damaged the median nerve, so jerking the thumb across the palm of the hand. Here was the explanation of why the thumbs were absent in the images on the Shroud. These two discoveries, the

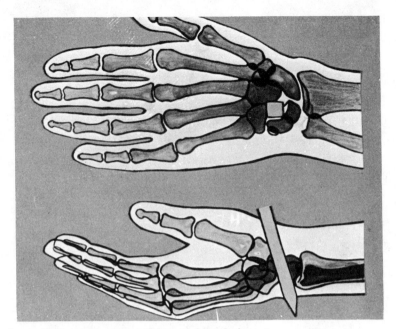

Plate 13 Below: The passage of the nail through the wrist

use of the wrists for nailing and the movement of the thumbs, were, for reasons we examined earlier, resounding proofs that the stains could not have been painted on the cloth.

When Barbet was conducting his research, no remains of any crucified victims had as yet been discovered. In 1968, however, when the foundations of a building were being dug in Jerusalem, one such victim was found. From the name in the tomb it is believed he was called Jehohanan. His bones were found with those of a child in one of the ossuaries in three burial caves on the site. The remains were in a poor state, but Dr Nicu Haas, of the Department of Anatomy, Hebrew University-Hadassah Medical School, and his colleagues were able to separate Jehohanan's bones from those of the child and make sure that they were the only two.

Jehohanan had been in his mid twenties, and a healthy man, but there were three signs of violence on his bones. First, a large nail went straight through his heel bones, and the tip of the nail was bent and had tough knobs of olive wood attached to it. Apparently the nail had been deformed on hitting a knot in the wood, and this had made it so difficult to draw out that the executioner

45

had simply hacked out the chunk of wood and cut off the feet, putting the lot in the ossuary.

The second injury was found on a bone of the forearm. A scratch and other signs on it suggested that his arms had been nailed to the cross-bar above the wrist bones, between the radius and ulna. The last set of injuries was severe fractures on the lower leg bones, and there is no doubt that these had resulted from the deliberate smashing of the man's legs to bring his life to an end.

As for the date of Jehohanan's death, it is estimated as having occurred between A.D. 7 and 70. Whatever the reason for his melancholy end, it is encouraging to find that the first material remains should conform in so many respects with the written descriptions of crucifixions which were the only previous evidence.

Barbet also did some interesting research into the bloodstains on the shroud. He carefully measured the angle between the two trickles from the wound on the wrist, and estimated the exact position of the body on the cross when it was pressing up on the feet and when it was slumped. He studied the stains closely, coming to the conclusion they were all from fresh and moist clots, with the exception of that from below the foot, which had been liquid blood. Even the trickle round the back of the body from the wound in the side had clotted slightly by the time the body had been laid in the Shroud – there are apparently signs of plenty of serum round the marks. How the newly clotted blood transferred to the material he could not be certain, and nobody has yet demonstrated it convincingly, but perhaps the moisture on the body kept the blood clots as a fairly moist paste, or perhaps some component in the material partially dissolved them on contact.

It was this question of the freshness of the blood which first interested me. I had read a suggestion that blood only flows from wounds when the heart is beating, and that Jesus was therefore still alive when taken down from the Cross, in a book called *Inquest on Jesus Christ* by John Reban. Should this move any readers to obtain a copy, they ought first to read the article by Dr David Willis in the *Ampleforth Journal* (Spring 1969), which reveals the true credentials of Reban, alias Naber, alias Berna, and also points out some of the medical inaccuracies the book contains.

Initially, I took the book at its face value, accepting the statement on the cover that Reban was the 'world's foremost authority on the Holy Shroud'. Looking at the photographs in the book, it seemed obvious that blood had been flowing when the Shroud was applied, especially from the jagged stain on the cloth near the right foot. Did this mean the body was certainly alive then, as the book stated, quoting apparently trustworthy names of medical authorities? Could Jesus therefore have recovered in the tomb, walked out naked, leaving the grave-linen behind, and put on the gardener's clothes which had been left in a shed? The book claimed that such a theory was revealed partly as an inspired vision. It all seemed very odd, and as a practising Christian I felt I had to find out if there was any truth in the theory.

I wrote off for, and obtained, some large positive and negative photographs of the Shroud. I then telephoned the local police. I told them I had photographic evidence of a terrible crime and that I wished to have my suspicions confirmed before making any accusations. To my considerable pleasure they gave me the telephone number of the East Midlands Forensic Laboratory in Nottingham, which is close to my home.

When I rang the laboratory I was answered by Mr Norman Lee, the head of the division. He was more canny than the police had been, asking what evidence existed on the photographs, including what wounds were visible and how I thought the person had died. Then, as I feared might happen, his suspicious voice asked when I thought the crime had taken place.

'About two thousand years ago,' I had to answer, fearing he would slam the phone down, but I went on quickly to give him enough information to arouse his interest. It worked, and he kindly invited me to bring the photographs round to the laboratory later in the week.

He met me at the door on to the car park, and led me up the stairs to a large laboratory. There I was rather surprised when the six or seven scientists, who had been working at various benches round the room, left their work to gather round a large flat table near one end, and Mr Lee led me to join them. They all seemed rather jovial, and it had not occurred to me that forensic scientists would be light-hearted by nature. When I left, three hours later, Mr Lee confessed to me that he had told them someone who sounded like 'a first-class crank' was coming round and that they might be amused to hear what he had to say.

Their attitude changed as soon as I placed the large photographs on the table. The image of the face in the negative is always immediately impressive to people who have never seen it before. I was invited to describe what was known about the Shroud, the reasons why it could not have been forged and how we can be confident that the body it contained had been that of Jesus Christ. They followed the arguments carefully, examining the details in the photographs, and confirmed all the deductions made and such points as the possibility of ammonia from the decomposing urea in the sweat having developed the stains in the first place.

Soon it was my turn to ask questions, and I started with the main one which had brought me to see them. Was the fact that blood was flowing from the wounds when the body was brought down from the Cross proof that the heart was still beating?

Apparently it was not. Blood drains from the wounds of dead bodies through gravity, and while very little may have been above the wound in the foot, for instance, it takes only a small amount of blood to make a lot of stain. However, they would like to have had more details as to how Barbet had distinguished between the clotted and the fresh blood, and this I was unable to give them. Soon after death, they pointed out, blood tends to separate into cells and serum, and they would have liked to see the stains on the Shroud closely before giving a further opinion. For the moment, on the evidence available, they could only say that the body might have been dead.

I asked them about rigor mortis next, for if the Shroud gave evidence for it, then the body must have been dead. In Rinaldi's book *The Man in the Shroud* it says that not even a present-day artist would have had the knowledge and skill to paint an image showing so clearly 'the perfect characteristics of a corpse in the condition of rigor mortis, with the added characteristics of one who died while hanging by the arms, such as the abnormally expanded rib case, the distended lower abdomen, the sharply drawn in epigastric hollow . . .' This description had interested me. Why should rigor mortis have preserved the position of the chest on the Cross, but have allowed the arms to be folded down?

Rigor mortis, it was clear from their discussion, is not a simple subject. They spiced their argument with gruesome examples at frequent intervals, and to a non-medical man like myself it all became somewhat harrowing. I could not help wondering whether, away from their work, they could resist emphasizing points which came up in social conversation with grisly illustrations. Perhaps their families and friends became hardened to such grim anecdotes.

There had been a case just recently when a man had died at about midnight with one arm stuck out at right angles to his body, not unlike the position of the arms in crucifixion. They had been to collect the body the next day, and rigor was complete. They had forced the body into the usual plastic wrapper, and laced it up really tight, but as they were taking it away they had had a nasty turn as, with a sudden wrenching, tearing sound, the arm had shot back into its previous position.

Did this mean, I had to ask, that it was impossible to have rigor mortis preserving the expanded chest but allowing the arms to be folded in?

Well, once again, rigor mortis is a complicated subject. It starts at the extremities and works its way to the centre of the body, and then it works its way out again in the same order. For instance, there was this case of the fellow who threw himself off Clifton Bridge . . .

It remained difficult to get specific answers on this point, but what they would commit themselves to was to say that you can only tell rigor mortis has set in by feeling the body. There was no way in which the Shroud could have given evidence of rigor mortis to prove the body was dead. In any case, there was the question of time. Jesus could not, according to the Gospel accounts, have been dead longer than three hours when placed in the tomb; probably the time was shorter, so rigor could not have started, or would only have been affecting the extremities, such as the end of the nose, the lips and the finger-tips. They referred to Taylor's *Principles and Practice of Medical Jurisprudence*, which is the forensic scientist's gospel (or perhaps it may be better described in the present work as the forensic equivalent of the medical student's Gray's *Anatomy*). There it stated quite specifically that rigor mortis sets in between three and six hours after death. Even this caused a difference of opinion. There was the instance of the woman who . . . But her case did not affect the basic agreement that the Shroud could not show the passage of rigor mortis, and therefore could not prove that the body was absolutely dead.

I then asked them the direct question. On the evidence of the photographs, did they think that the body in the Turin Shroud had been alive or dead?

They discussed this at considerable length, realizing, of course, that a verdict of alive would have considerable implications. But there was one feature of the photographs which they could not equate with a normal dead body: the evenness of the stains.

As soon as the heart stops beating, the blood stops circulating and the skin temperature starts to vary considerably from place to place. They quoted a case that had happened not long before. A woman had died soon after getting out of her bath, and her naked body had fallen partly across the tiled bathroom floor and partly across the carpeted floor outside. Such was the temperature difference quickly established, that by the time she was found half of her body was almost black with decomposition while the rest was still white. The evenness of the stains in the Shroud is therefore a problem. Whether the agent developing the stains had been ammonia, moisture or whatever, the darkness of the stain at any point must have depended on the strength of the developing agent and the temperature of the cloth at that point. With the wide differences in surface temperature that would have developed in a dead body, the stains could be expected to vary enormously. It was not just a case of what that part of the body was resting on and how well it conducted heat, as in the example of the woman on the conducting tiles and the insulating carpet; the rate at which any part of the body loses heat depends on its surface area, whereas the quantity of heat it contains depends on its volume and what is inside it. One would expect to see signs of lividity if the body had been dead, for just this reason. In a dead body, the blood quickly descends to the lowest points because of gravity, so one would expect signs of this under the buttocks and shoulder-blades, since the blood would have increased the thermal capacity of those areas and the temperature would have taken longer to drop to the ambient temperature.

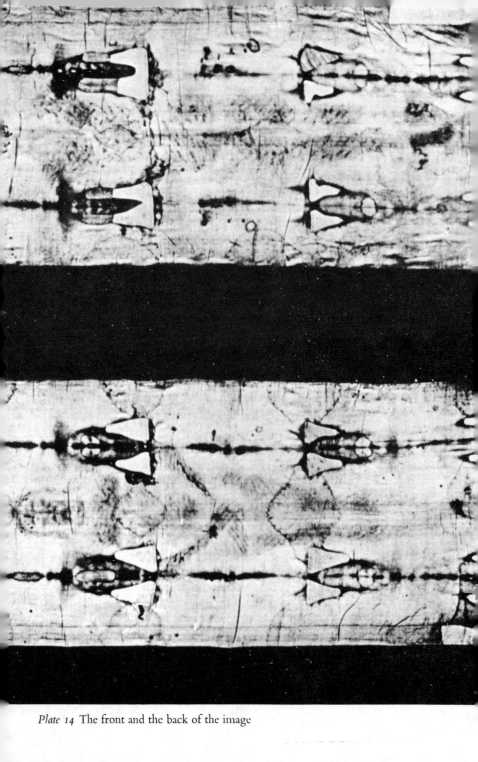

Plate 14 The front and the back of the image

No, they said: on balance, the body in the Shroud was still just alive by twentieth-century standards.

I pointed to the lance-wound. Could he have survived that? They examined the point of entry, not far below the arm-pit.

If you put your finger on the spot, and then raised your arm up to above the horizontal as in the slumped position on the cross, the spot moved quite a bit higher, so that it was most unlikely that the heart would have been pierced. That wound should not have been fatal. As for the mixture of water and blood, which Barbet thought must have confirmed that the pericardium, part of the heart, must have been pierced, this was not so. St John's account may well be right for quite another reason. As a result of the tortures suffered there would have been congestion of the lung bases and a simple pleural effusion; in other words, a watery liquid would have interposed between the lungs and the thoracic cage. When the lance pierced the side, this liquid would have been released, mixing with blood from the wound to give the effect recorded by St John. The liquid may even have pushed the lungs out of the way of the wound, so that when the liquid was tapped the lung could have expanded to fill the space again entirely uninjured. Even if the lung had been pierced, lungs are extremely tolerant of injury and can localize the damage to one part without allowing the whole to be affected. And the wound could seal itself. It might have been helped in this by the myrrh on the linen, since myrrh has been known for years for its curative properties, and tincture of myrrh may still be bought in chemist's shops today as a treatment for mouth ulcers.

The lance wound was therefore unlikely to have caused death by present-day standards. On the other hand, it was absolute as a proof of death by the standards of the first century. At that time the lungs were regarded as the centre of life, and if breathing stopped, this was the sign of death; the body had given up the ghost. If the form of death prevented the ghost, or spirit of life, from departing from the lungs, as in strangulation or drowning for instance, the body was unclean, and Jews were not allowed to eat the meat of animals that had died in this way.

Recognition of death varies with the increase in knowledge, and we must keep in mind in our present study that it was quite possible for Jesus to have been absolutely dead by first-century standards, even though he may not have died by ours. Present-day standards may well be a long way wrong to future generations. Some rich Americans are having their bodies deep-frozen on death in the hope that future technology will be able to restore them to life. If that happens, the generation accomplishing this will know these people to be alive, even though we have correctly considered them to be dead.

Even when the definition of death is known, the borderline between life and death is often difficult to determine. There are a number of cases each year of bodies, certified dead by competent doctors, coming alive again to contradict their judgement. Mistakes are easily made.

Perhaps it would seem surprising for the Roman soldiers to have made a mistake, however. They were hardened campaigners, and had probably been present at many crucifixions and had plenty of practice at recognizing dead bodies – but bodies dead by the standards of their own time. How did they recognize death? Probably by the lack of any movement, including the motion of breathing. They would have been certain, after two or three hours, that Jesus was dead by those standards, and to make sure there could be no mistake, they confirmed it by piercing his lungs which were the centre of life.

How then, I asked the forensic scientists, could he have satisfied the Romans and the burial party that he was dead, and yet have remained alive?

He probably sank into a coma.

There are many ifs and buts to any theory, for crucifixion has not been practised since Roman times and the medical details are not known. Historical reports tell us, however, that death on the cross was a slow business, and that there was a gradual decline. There were cases of people recovering when taken down after a considerable time on the cross, and one such is mentioned by Josephus in his autobiography:

And when I was sent by Titus Caesar with Cerealius, and a thousand horsemen, to a certain village called Thecoa, in order to know whether it were a place fit for a camp, as I came back, I saw many captives crucified, and remembered three of them as my former acquaintance. I was very sorry at this in my mind,

53

and went with tears in my eyes to Titus, and told him of them; so he immediately commanded them to be taken down, and to have the greatest care taken of them in order to their recovery; yet two of them died under the physician's hands, while the third recovered. [IV: 75]

The punishment which their bodies were apparently able to withstand is astonishing, particularly as it was apparently normal practice to flog the prisoner severely before crucifying him.

With Jesus, however, it was not a long-drawn-out end. The signs of death came very suddenly, after about three hours on the Cross, and the bystanders and Pilate were surprised at its abruptness. There was none of the usual slow decline. Just before his death he was talking naturally to his mother and St John, and all four Gospels say he gave a final cry as he died, which could not have happened after the start of a terminal heart attack.

The Shroud has confirmed so many of the precise details which are recorded in the Gospels' descriptions of the event, that we may regard with considerable confidence other reports that the Shroud cannot confirm. For instance, the three Synoptic Gospels record the Aramaic version as well as the translation of the cry, 'My God, my God, why hast thou forsaken me?' And there is another reason why we can be sure it is true, which I will mention later. Moreover, all four of them describe one extraordinary incident: a Roman soldier offering vinegar to Jesus. St Luke then mentions a brief conversation with the penitent thief in between, but the other three go from this straight to the final cry and death. Were the two connected? Why was the vinegar offered? As St John's account is probably that of an eyewitness, we will give it precedence:

> After that, Jesus, aware that all had now come to its appointed end, said in fulfilment of Scripture, 'I thirst.' A jar stood there full of sour wine; so they soaked a sponge with the wine, fixed it on a javelin, and held it up to his lips. Having received the wine, he said, 'It is accomplished!' He bowed his head and gave up his spirit. [19: 28–30]

The Romans used to flavour their drinking water with vinegar. They may have had a pot of neat vinegar to hand as well as pots of water. It may be that a Roman soldier offered a sponge dipped in vinegar as an extra torture to the thirsty Jesus. He would have had to cough and splutter it out, and it may have been the last trial he was capable of enduring. Crying, 'It is finished!' he may have slumped down in a dead faint. He would then barely have been able to breathe in the collapsed position, and he may have entered into a comatose state. If so, his breathing would have slowed to a barely perceptible rhythm, probably only diaphragmatic and entirely invisible to a normal observer. His body temperature would have lowered, his heartbeat have run down, his blood pressure have lowered and his legs have swollen with fluid draining to them. His skin would have gone an ashen colour and have been clammy with perspiration. So he would have hung, and the Romans, used to the rapid death of prisoners as soon as they could no longer press up on their legs and seeing no sign of breathing, would have felt sure that he was dead. It was probably in this condition, not unlike a state of hibernation or the trance in which fakirs can be buried alive for long periods, that he was pierced by the lance, taken down from the Cross, carried the short distance to the tomb and left covered in the Shroud.

This was not the end, I pointed out to the forensic experts. Could he therefore have recovered from the coma while in the tomb?

Possibly.

And could he have pushed away the stone and emerged on his own?

No, unless by supernatural powers. It is true that no bones had been broken and that the wounds were mainly superficial. True also that people make remarkably quick recoveries and some-times discharge themselves from hospital shortly after being very badly injured. For instance, there was a case only the other day of a man who . . . But for the body in the Shroud, the shock to the system must have been terrible. He would have needed two or three weeks of tender care and nursing to be brought back to health.

And that, they implied, was a problem they could not help me solve.

6 CUSTODIANS OF THE TOMB

By sunset on Friday, as the Sabbath began, the body of Jesus had been placed in the tomb by Joseph of Arimathea and Nicodemus, and covered with the shroud Joseph had bought. The tomb was new and unused. Some of the women disciples of Jesus had followed the burial party, so also knew where the tomb was, and since they had seen that the burial was temporary, 'went home and prepared spices and perfumes; and on the Sabbath they rested in obedience to the commandment' (Luke 23: 56). The tomb was sealed with a large stone, but left unguarded, and the body inside was in a deep coma. By Sunday morning the body had gone.

Only one of the Gospels mentions the placing of a guard on the tomb: that of St Matthew. Whether this was historically true is open to doubt, as it may well have been written by the evangelist to counter rumours that the body was taken away by disciples. Nevertheless it is possible the author of Matthew had a special source for his story, and if the word reached Caiaphas and the chief priests on the Saturday morning that the body had not, as they presumed, been thrown into the communal grave which was the responsibility of the Roman soldiers, but removed to an unguarded grave by a Jew, a member of the governing council, the Sanhedrin, they would probably have acted exactly as Matthew describes:

Plate 15 The sepulchre prepared for Joseph of Arimathea may have looked like this – a large stone runs along a gully to seal the entrance

Next day, the morning after that Friday, the chief priests and the Pharisees came in a body to Pilate. 'Your Excellency,' they said, 'we recall how that impostor said while he was still alive, "I am to rise after three days." So will you give orders for the grave to be made secure until the third day? Otherwise his disciples may come, steal the body, and then tell the people that he has been raised from the dead; and the final deception will be worse than the first.' 'You may have your guard,' said Pilate; 'go and make it secure as best you can.' So they went and made the grave secure; they sealed the stone, and left the guard in charge. [Matthew 27: 62–6]

This meant, apparently, that Pilate refused the use of Roman troops for the guard, so the chief priests had to use some of the Temple Watch. It is a measure of how great they thought the risk of Jesus's disappearance that they were willing to defile themselves by going to the sepulchre, and on the Sabbath as well. They must have been very relieved on opening the tomb to see the body still there in the Shroud (had the stains developed much by then, one wonders?), and they must have been much happier once they had sealed the grave and left the men to protect it.

Yet, by the Sunday morning, the stone had been rolled back, the tomb left empty and the guards gone. What had happened?

The explanation Matthew gives is one of the sections that rings less convincingly as fact:

Suddenly there was a violent earthquake; an angel of the Lord descended from heaven; he came to the stone and rolled it away, and sat himself down on it. His face shone like lightning; his garments were white as snow. At the sight of him the guards shook with fear and lay like the dead. [28: 2–4]

Others may believe it, but when nothing has so far broken normal physical laws, I feel unwilling at this stage to accept a supernatural explanation such as an angel pushing back the stone. There must be a rational explanation.

Now, opening the sealed tomb and pushing back the stone would have needed several men, for the stone was probably a massive circular one running along a gulley. We know how the women were worried about it: 'They were wondering among themselves who would roll away the stone for them from the entrance to the tomb, when they looked up and saw that the stone, huge as it was, had been rolled back already' (Mark 16: 3f.). It must surely have been done by the guard. But why would they have wanted to enter the tomb?

My own feeling is that if there really was a guard, they might have been tempted to enter the tomb to rob it. The vast quantity of myrrh and aloes brought by Nicodemus, more than half a hundredweight (John 19: 39), must have been worth a fortune. Nicodemus is reputed to have been very rich indeed, but even so, the amount recorded seems extraordinarily excessive. To the soldiers, accompanying the chief priests in their tour of inspection on the Saturday morning, the sight of that quantity, and the thought of what it would have cost, may well have aroused their cupidity. In the long hours of uneventful watching, a plan hesitantly suggested by one of them for removing some of the spices, perhaps replacing them with earth in the bottom of the jar and selling them for a great deal of money, could have hardened into a firm resolve for joint action. After all, why leave all that money rotting in the earth and of no use to anyone? And nobody could possibly tell if the jar looked as full as before and only the top was covered with the spices.

If they did resolve to rob the tomb, the dead of night was the natural time to choose – perhaps two or three hours before sunrise on the Sunday morning. With the aid of flares or flickering oil lamps, they would have forced back the great stone at the entrance and have gone into the outer chamber. There would have been an inner recess leading off it, and on a ledge at the side would have rested the body in its Shroud, while the spices were probably in a large jar on the floor. They only had to go into the recess to take them.

Yet they fled. Why?

It may have had to do with the Shroud, and the fact that the body was in a coma. They would have been frightened by the risk they were taking, for to be caught could have cost them their lives, or at least have earned a very severe flogging. The surroundings must have been unnerving in any case, and their flickering lamps would have sent distorted shadows dancing on the roughly hewn walls. Then, again, it was no ordinary person lying there dead. As members of the Temple Watch they would have known a lot about him. They must have been extremely apprehensive, and in those circumstances it would have taken only one frightening incident to send them running in terror.

Perhaps it was the Shroud that did it, for the material is so thin that the stains go right through, and by the light of their torches, particularly if the head had been pillowed up to face them, the negative image of the face apparently staring at them might have started the panic. Perhaps they suddenly noticed the cloth slowly moving in and out in front of the nose, because of the minimal breathing. The body could even have jerked in its coma, or the smoke from the torches could have made it cough. Any one such incident, I suggest, could have been horrifying, and could be enough to explain their desertion of the tomb.

There is another possible explanation which does not involve the body or the Shroud. Suppose, after they had opened the tomb and most of them had gone in, the ones left outside on watch suddenly saw a party approaching in the moonlight, coming straight up the hill from Jerusalem. They would have no time to roll back the stone; caught red-handed, they could not have concealed the fact that they had intended to rob the tomb they were guarding. This, too, might have caused them to flee, and to cover themselves they invented the story about the earthquake and the angel later incorporated in St Matthew's Gospel. The last part of the story, as narrated by Matthew, may be absolutely true:

> . . . Some of the guard went into the city and reported to the chief priests everything that had happened. After meeting with the elders and conferring together, the chief priests offered the soldiers a substantial bribe and told them to say, 'His disciples came by night and stole the body while we were asleep.' They added, 'If this should reach the Governor's ears, we will put matters right with him and see that you do not suffer.' So they took the money and did as they were told. This story became widely known, and is current in Jewish circles to this day. [Matthew 28: 11–15]

Their lie paid off, handsomely. They can hardly have believed their luck.

But such speculation on the story in Matthew about what happened to the custodians of the tomb is no more than a side-issue. The question which really matters is what became of the body of Jesus?

7 THE RESURRECTION

The Resurrection is the foundation stone on which the Christian Church is built, and it is surprising, indeed most disappointing, that the Gospel accounts of the event itself, and the post-Resurrection appearances, do not reflect this. They are remarkably brief and, in some ways, contradictory. We will consider this in more detail later on.

For the moment there are three points which a direct study of the Gospels reveals. First, the actual Resurrection was not witnessed by any of the disciples. None of the Gospels records it. In a way, this is quite a convincing argument for their truth, for an imaginative author would have been unable to resist describing it as the crucial point of the whole story. Secondly, soon after sunrise on the Sunday morning, when Mary Magdalene came to the tomb alone (John) or accompanied by other women disciples (the Synoptics), the tomb was empty. The body had gone. And lastly, the body of Jesus in the post-Resurrection appearances was a completely physical one.

The first two conclusions will probably be accepted straight away. The third needs amplification. Consider, for instance, Luke:

As they were talking about all this, there he was, standing among them. Startled and terrified, they thought they were seeing a ghost. But he said, 'Why are you so perturbed? Why do questionings arise in your minds? Look at my hands and feet. It is I myself. Touch me and see; no ghost has flesh and bones as you can see that I have.' They were still unconvinced, still wondering, for it seemed too good to be true. So he asked them, 'Have you anything here to eat?' They offered him a piece of fish they had cooked, which he took and ate before their eyes. [Luke 24: 36–43]

This was no phantom. A hallucination of this sort is unlikely to be experienced by a whole group of people in the same way simultaneously, and no insubstantial spirit would be able to eat fish. St John's Gospel emphasizes the solidity of Jesus in the same way, as in the section where he encourages Thomas to feel the wounds in his hands and side.

Against these descriptions of a very physical being must be set statements that he entered through locked doors and disappeared from their company equally mysteriously. This, again, will be discussed later.

The evidence of the Shroud is that the body lay in it in a coma, though not long enough for decomposition to mar the stains, yet was in no condition to leave it unaided. We must combine this with the written evidence of the Gospels that the Resurrection was physical, that the body and Shroud had gone from the tomb by the Sunday morning, and that none of the disciples whose memories formed the traditions of the early Church witnessed the Resurrection.

The only logical explanation seems to be that the body and Shroud were removed from the tomb during Saturday night, and by someone or some people who were not known by those disciples. And then, given a little further thought, the suspicion grows that the two people who knew where the tomb was and had a reason for returning to it, and who were not on speaking terms with the other disciples, were Joseph of Arimathea and Nicodemus.

The idea that they took the body from the tomb is a very ancient one: almost two thousand years old, in fact. If you are interested, you can read of the trial of Joseph of Arimathea on that charge in the book in the New Testament Apocrypha called the Acts of Pilate or the Gospel of Nicodemus. Though of doubtful authorship and date, it may well be based on genuine tradition, and the courage of Joseph at the trial shines through the account.

While the suggestion was mooted long ago, it has been considered to have a central weakness in that no one has thought of a really sound motive for Joseph of Arimathea to move the body. The most likely hypothesis was that, since the tomb had been recently made for his own body (Matthew 27: 60), he put the body of Jesus in it just as a temporary measure, and wanted to move it out to another, permanent grave as soon as possible. In his book *Who Moved the Stone?*, F. Morison analyses this fully. Among other considerations he cites the fact that, as a sympathizer who had bravely displayed his respect for Jesus by asking for his body, Joseph is most unlikely to have wanted to move it from his tomb. If, however, he had done so, he would probably have transferred the body by day, and the true facts would in any case have been easily found out by the priests. Also, the new tomb would have quickly become an object of veneration.

The arguments, which should be read in full in that fascinating book, are quite convincing, but the Shroud itself suggests a quite different motive for Joseph's removing the body, and one which makes the whole pattern fall into place and looks much more probable.

We need now to go over the situation carefully.

To begin with, we must realize just how astonishingly brave and unselfish Joseph had been in asking for the body. The Pontius Pilate of the Gospels is a hard but just man, who did his best to make sure that Jesus had a fair trial, but in the end gave in to the mob as he was afraid he would be reported to Rome. Search other accounts and a different picture emerges. In Josephus, for instance, all his actions are those of an unsympathetic and vicious tyrant. In Philo, the characteristics of his government are described as 'his corruptions, his acts of insolence, his rapine, and his habit of insulting people, his cruelty, and his continual murders of people untried and uncondemned, and his never-ending, gratuitous, and most grievous inhumanity'. He does not sound the sort of man you would happily approach for a favour. Moreover, in doing so, Joseph was openly expressing his sympathy for the disgraced and crucified prophet, and was thereby ruining his career, risking his life, and bringing on his head the hostility of his friends and those in authority.

Having taken this astonishingly brave step, Joseph was prevented, by the onset of the Sabbath, from accomplishing more than a temporary burial. Surely he could not have left the job unfinished, having given up so much to start it? Now that he had openly and irrevocably associated himself with Jesus's cause, he had nothing more to lose by completing the Jewish rites on the body.

So it might in fact be thought extraordinary if he had not gone back to wash, anoint and bind the body. What is most surprising in the Gospel accounts is that the women, having seen Joseph give the body only a temporary burial, should have thought he would not return to complete the task.

The omission of Nicodemus so far is deliberate. Nicodemus is thought by some to have been invented by John for a literary reason, but this seems unlikely. A Nicodemus is mentioned in the Talmud as being so wealthy that he could have fed the whole population of Israel for ten days, and it may be the same man. He had the contract for supplying water to the Temple, and was still living at the time of the fall of Jerusalem in A.D. 70. He would have been fairly young, therefore, at the time when he went to Jesus by night, and though his question in the Sanhedrin (John 7: 51) implies a measure of courage, we need not be surprised that he lacked the audacity to accompany Joseph to Pilate. Not until Joseph had, remarkably, been granted permission to bury the body did Nicodemus find the courage to join him openly, and the fact that he brought the enormous quantity of spices is proof, surely, that together they were expecting to complete the rites as soon as the end of the Sabbath allowed it.

Next we have to decide when they would have done it, and some time during Saturday night seems probable. First, they would not have wanted the attention of a crowd, so would have waited for darkness to hide their activities. They may have hoped that their action would not reach the ears of the Sanhedrin, as the last straw, and Nicodemus, whose dread of hostile criticism from his friends or action by the Sanhedrin had caused him to visit Jesus by night before, would have wanted to go by night again. There is another reason why they would not have waited until dawn.

Decomposition sets in rapidly in the Palestinian climate, and so even today the Jews and Mohammedans of the area bury their dead within twenty-four hours. The unaccompanied women had to wait for the light to move, but not Joseph and Nicodemus.

Passover always coincides with the full moon, so they would probably have needed no other light before reaching the tomb. It is possible, as suggested in the previous chapter, that they arrived in time to catch the guard in the act of robbing the tomb and caused them to flee in panic – even more likely if the new-comers were recognized as elders. The name of the hill Golgotha, which means 'a skull', implies a convex shape, so the guard may not have been able to watch much of the slope in keeping a lookout. However, it is just as likely that they found the tomb deserted. To enter it they would have had to light a flaming torch or an oil lamp, using tinder and steel.

The exact rites for burying the dead are not known for certain, but they probably included washing the corpse (Acts 9:37) and anointing it with perfume and oil (John 12: 7; Mark 16: 1) before winding it in linen clothes containing spices (John 19: 40). The hands and feet were bound together, as were the cheekbones (John 11: 44).

Entering the inner recess of the tomb, prepared to carry out the initial washing, they would have stripped back the top of the Shroud, expecting to find a completely cold and lifeless corpse, still, they hoped, unaffected by decomposition. Up to now, I think, they would have had no motive for removing the body. But it would not have been as they expected. The body temperature, which on the Friday evening had been colder than the thundery atmosphere – in any case, they would have expected the body to have lost heat slowly – was now considerably higher than the temperature of the tomb. The face, too, was in repose, on the evidence of the stains in the Shroud, rather than showing the staring, open-jawed vacuity they would have expected. They would have looked more closely and have noticed, probably, other signs that seemed strange in a body they knew had died, including faint signs of breathing.

What would they have done then? Discussing the matter in the tomb, they would have recalled Jesus's prophecy, well known in Jerusalem, that he would rebuild the Temple (subsequently interpreted as his body) in three days and nights. This would have explained its strange state. It would have been foolish, therefore, to bind it up tight as they would a corpse, so giving Jesus the additional barrier of bonds to break as he recovered. Lazarus, after all, had had to be released from his wrappings. It would also have been unwise to leave him unguarded in the open tomb. Better surely to take him somewhere where he could be guarded, tended and watched until he recovered. Here was the motive for taking the body away. When the chief priests offered the members of the guard a substantial bribe to spread the lie that 'His disciples came by night and stole the body', it was in fact the truth.

Most likely Joseph and Nicodemus took the body to one of their houses to recover – probably Nicodemus's rather than Joseph's since he was not under the same suspicion – and their positions would have meant they would have kept the secret to themselves and perhaps one or two others whom they could trust implicitly.

There were practical details to solve, but they were not insuperable. For instance, the business of carrying the body may have been accomplished on a bier, which consisted then of a flat board supported by two or three staves; and there were probably one or two handy which the Romans used to carry the bodies of crucified victims to the communal grave. Then, again, in hiding him in a private house, they may have been helped by the fact that many houses in Jersualem had an upper room, separate from the rest of the accommodation, for the use of visitors during the three great religious festivals of the year.

About the recovery of the body, the forensic scientists told me that it could have come round at any time; but it would then have needed two or three weeks at least of careful nursing to allow the wounds to heal. By then, although the scars would still have shown on the wrists, feet and side, Jesus could have been fit to go and find his disciples who had been scattered like sheep (Mark 14: 27). This could have happened. Here is the answer to Strauss, who up to now has struck the flaw in rational explanations:

> It is impossible that a being who had stolen half-dead out of the sepulchre, weak and ill, wanting treatment and bandaging, could have given the disciples the impression that he was the

conqueror of the death and the grave, the Prince of life; an impression that lay at the bottom of their future ministry. Such a resuscitation could only have weakened the impression which he had made upon them in life and in death.

By the time he would have found them – poor, dispirited men, certain of his death and burial – he would have been perfectly alive physically, with the scars to prove it was indeed the resurrected body of their master. Is it any wonder that such a conviction changed them into the men they became?

8   THE EYEWITNESS

It was the overall evenness of the stains which suggested to the forensic scientists that the body was in a coma, the heart still beating, while in the Shroud. The fact that the stains were not ruined by the onset of decomposition meant that the body must have been removed from the Shroud by someone within about thirty-six hours. Hence my proposal that Joseph and Nicodemus took it.

When one moves from the general impression of the stains to a more detailed examination of them, there is a lot of information available already, most notably in the book by Dr Pierre Barbet called *A Doctor at Calvary*. Here a surgeon's analysis, apart from the major discovery of the nailing of the wrists in crucifixion already referred to, gives minute details of the scourging and beating the body had suffered, the type of cross used, the carrying on the shoulders of the cross-bar or *patibulum*, the two body positions on the Cross and the crown of thorns. He found, too, how the marks showed that, to remove the body from the Cross, the nail through the feet had been removed from the upright, and the body then lowered, still attached to the cross-bar. It was carried to the tomb before the nails were removed, two people holding the beam, one the ankles, and two a twisted piece of sheet passed under the trunk.

His account is detailed and fascinating, and presumably a close examination of the Shroud by other surgeons would confirm these conclusions. The most impressive feature of the book is the way it conveys with horrific realism the agonies and tortures endured by Jesus.

There are grounds for three slight reservations about the book, however. First, Barbet was intensely religious, so he was bound to view the story from the angle prescribed by his faith. Secondly, and this follows partly from the former point, the medical details are made to fit the assumption that Jesus died absolutely, by twentieth-century standards, on the Cross, so that he gives lengthy arguments about the cause of death and does not consider seriously whether the body was actually dead. This, in turn, affects his argument about the lance-wound, which he has entering the heart, and the draining of the dead blood from the body on the way to the tomb. Thirdly, he is apt to skirt round problems he cannot answer. For example, he is happy to explain how Joseph and Nicodemus left the materials for completing the burial rites in the tomb, and goes straight on to say that the women disciples came to complete the task on the Sunday morning. There are other places, particularly involving the Shroud and the grave-linen in the tomb, where one senses a skilful avoidance of difficulties. Nevertheless it is a book which everyone interested in the Shroud should read.

The opinion of the forensic scientists that the body must have been taken from the tomb in a coma threw an entirely new light on the written evidence. Piecing it together, the idea that Joseph and Nicodemus took the body away began to answer several problems in the Gospel accounts which had previously looked insoluble. Snags remained, however. Some were slowly unravelled by further study of the Shroud and the written accounts, while other aspects still remain puzzling.

Three problems in particular needed to be unravelled. In the first place, there was St John's eyewitness account of the linen in the tomb. Secondly, there were the times of the post-Resurrection appearances: according to the Gospels, these started on the day the tomb was found empty, for it was on that day that Jesus is reported to have appeared to Mary Magdalene and the disciples on the road to Emmaus. The third puzzling feature was the supernatural element in the reports of the post-Resurrection appearances: such things as the way Jesus appeared suddenly among his disciples though the doors were locked (John 20: 19), and then left just as mysteriously.

The passage in St John which, for quite a large number of people, provides the main stumbling-block to the acceptance of the Shroud as genuine, tells how John and Peter, the two disciples, were running to the tomb, and John reached it first:

> He peered in and saw the linen wrappings lying there, but did not enter. Then Simon Peter came up, following him, and he went into the tomb. He saw the linen wrappings lying, and the napkin which had been over his head, not lying with the wrappings but rolled together in a place by itself. Then the disciple who had reached the tomb first went in too, and he saw and believed . . . [John 20: 5–8]

The question arises, how can this account be made to accord with the description in the Synoptics of the *sindon*, or Shroud; or with the evidence of the Holy Shroud itself, that the body that lay in it was unwashed and unbound when laid in the tomb? Up to now there has been no satisfactory explanation, even though a great deal of research has gone into trying to prove to the faithful that the Greek words for either napkin or wrappings can, under certain circumstances, mean a linen cloth such as a shroud. It is a weak argument, but since the faithful have been assured, first, that the relic is genuine by several Popes and that, secondly, St John's account is the uncompromising truth, the contradictions must be made to tally somehow. The argument suffers further, however, when St John also specifically states (19: 40) that the body was buried according to Jewish rites: in other words, washed, anointed and wrapped in linen. Yet even if we suppose that the wrappings or the napkin were in fact the Shroud rolled up, and that the images were formed by a release of energy as the body was supernaturally transmuted into a special resurrected state, who rolled the Shroud into the bundle? And what was the other pile?

It is possible that the words used in the English translation have influenced the way we interpret this passage, and Bishop John Robinson, in his book *The Human Face of God*, makes this observation:

The point is often made that the description of the grave-clothes in John 20: 5-7 is deliberately intended by the evangelist to discount robbery and give the impression that the body had been spirited out of them, leaving them undisturbed. But his Greek is so ambiguous as almost to suggest the opposite. It could perfectly naturally (if not most naturally) mean that the linen bands were 'lying about' and that the cloth that was 'over' (not round) the head had been 'rolled up' (or bundled together) '*into* one place'. This certainly would not *rule out* human interference. Clearly John does not intend the evidence to point this way, and it is the more significant, therefore, that he does not say, as Marxsen makes him say (!), that the clothes were 'neatly rolled together' and 'folded in an orderly fashion'.

At all events, there were two groups of grave-clothes lying separately, and neither was laid flat as the Shroud would have been had the body dematerialized within it. So we are still left with the fundamental contradiction between the Synoptic and John accounts. Can the Shroud help us to solve it?

The forensic experts pointed out that the stains were largely thermographic. This meant that, whatever the developing agent may have been, the density of the stain at any point had depended on the temperature and strength of the developing agent at that point. Because the stains were surprisingly even all over the body, the temperature was surprisingly constant and therefore the blood was circulating.

Bearing in mind the thermographic idea, it was possible to move on to consider various aspects of the stains. To begin with, the temperatures of the back and front of the body must have been similar. Therefore the losses of heat from the two surfaces must have been comparable; in fact, the loss from the bottom surface by conduction through the supporting ledge must have been about the same as that from the top surface through conduction and convection through the air, and perhaps a small amount of radiation. Could stone have been so poor a conductor? It is hard to say. There is a further complication. On a firm stone surface one would expect the back to be in contact with the cloth over fairly small areas, whereas almost all of the back has made close contact. The description of the tomb does not tell us

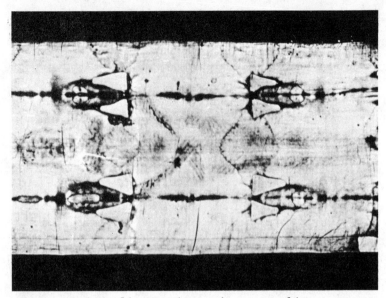

Plate 16 The back of the image showing the evenness of the stains, the darkness of the soles of the feet and the jagged bloodstain by the right heel

what the ledge was made of but it must either have been stone shaped to the contours of the body, or sand, or there may have been a covering of sorts which was insulating and pliable to the shape of the body placed on it. On the evidence, sand is the most likely answer, particularly as the Mishnah, the binding precepts of the Jewish elders codified in about A.D. 200, specifically states that a corpse may be laid out on sand, even on the Sabbath, so that it can be preserved longer.

This on its own would not explain the nature of the image of the feet. The soles, particularly the one of the right foot, were in contact with the cloth, and comparatively warm judging from the darkness of the stain. Since the body was horizontal, and the legs straight enough for the calves to rest on the cloth, the soles must have been nearly vertical. There was not apparently enough cloth to tuck up over the top of the feet, and even if it was at one time longer and had been trimmed at some point, simply tucking the cloth over the toes could not have kept so much of the soles warm and in contact. Something must have been pressing the Shroud against the feet; something soft and insulating.

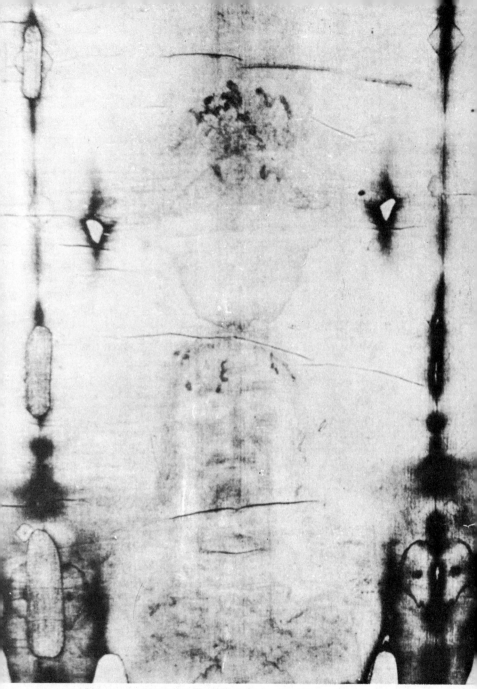

Plate 17 The head. The width of the stains indicate that there must have been a type of pillow to support it

The next area to consider is the back of the head. A convex shape resting on a plane surface would make contact at only one point, but the Shroud shows bloodstains, and the dark area made by body warmth, going right round the back of the head. Again, a soft, pliable material must have been present; a form of pillow, in fact. This is confirmed by the front image, for with nothing to support it the hair would have fallen below the ears, and the stains from the face would have been wider and more distorted. Even as it is, the narrowness of the image is a worrying feature, for the face is quite convex across normally, but with careful pillowing right round the side the hair could plausibly have been pressed against the cheek to give the result we see.

At this point I was left wondering what materials would have been available in the tomb to cushion the feet and head, when it struck me that this could be the answer to the contradiction between the Synoptics and St John's account. A possible explanation lay in the two piles of grave-linen. They could well have been left in place after Joseph and Nicodemus had taken the body away.

We know (Mark 15: 46) that Joseph bought the Shroud on the Friday evening for a temporary burial of the body because time was obviously going to be short. We also know (John 19: 39) that Nicodemus brought spices to the tomb on the evening they buried Jesus, ready for when they could carry out the full rites. Why the spices only, however, and not the grave-linen!

If he had taken the lot it would seem to make much more sense. Once they had wrapped the body temporarily in the Shroud, they would have seen where they could leave the other items in the tomb. The spices could go on the floor in their jar or other container, but they would not have dropped the grave-linen there; they would most likely have placed this on the ledge with the body. The most natural thing for them to do was then to pillow the head of the body of the master they revered as carefully and tenderly as possible. They would have placed some of the grave-linen underneath, and then more up the side of the head. (Barbet showed, incidentally, that the neck had been bent well forward, though he did not suggest why.) There was no doubt some material left over, and instead of smothering the top of the face they lifted the bottom of the Shroud against the soles of the feet, causing as they did so the jagged bloodstain we see beside the right foot, and adjusted the remaining bundle of grave-linen between it and the end of the ledge.

When they returned during the night and found the dead body in its strange condition, they would have lifted it off, possibly on to a form of stretcher, and have taken it away with the Shroud. Since they had enough to carry already, they left behind the spices, the grave-linen that had been round the head and pressing against the feet, to be discovered in exactly those positions by St John and St Peter.

The mistake the disciples made is perfectly understandable. John had been with the mother of Jesus at the Crucifixion. With almost his dying breath, Jesus had committed his mother to John's care. The time was about three o'clock. Shortly afterwards the last agony was over and Jesus had plainly died by the standards of the time, so John would have ushered Mary away from the harrowing sight of her dead son as quickly as possible. Three hours then remained before the Sabbath began. John could not have known of the time-wasting drama that followed, of Joseph's begging the body from Pilate, of the messages going back and forth between the Antonia fortress in Jerusalem and Golgotha outside it, and of the probable search for a place which would sell the materials on the day of Passover. He would have been ignorant of all this, and when he saw the two piles – the rolled-up napkin and linen as it appeared, with no body there – he concluded that they had been used on the body and that there had been time to prepare it properly. When he describes how, on the Sunday morning, Mary of Magdala went to the tomb, he gives no motive for her going. If he had been told by someone she had gone intending to wash and anoint the body, he would have disbelieved it; with his own eyes he had seen the evidence that the body had been properly buried.

It is interesting to speculate where St John might have heard of Nicodemus's part in the burial. Five people had carried the body to the tomb, and probably Joseph and Nicodemus had carried it away between them at night. One of the other three helpers may have been the source of John's information, telling him about Nicodemus, but it would be surprising, though not impossible, if he had not also mentioned that the burial was only temporary.

John, however, is quite specific. 'They took the body of Jesus and wrapped it, with the spices, in strips of linen cloth according to Jewish burial-customs' (19: 40). Even though he had the evidence of his eyes, if one of the helpers had told him that the burial was in a shroud on the Friday, would he have been so definite? Perhaps his certainty developed in time, for a further fifty or sixty years probably went by before he wrote his Gospel.

Turning back to the stains on the Shroud, there are other places where the thermographic evidence produces interesting implications, particularly on the face. The nose would have protruded far enough from the face for the cloth beside and below it to be held away from the skin, and so we would expect to find lighter stains at this point. In fact the stains are still quite dark, which may indicate warmth from minimal breathing, particularly since dark spots are visible on the moustache and beard just below the nose.

The density of the developing agent, whether it was a constituent of perspiration or simply moisture, must have played a considerable role in the staining. The kind loan by Philips Medical Services of a thermographic scanner enabled me to photograph the heat emitted by a human head. I chose a decidedly biblical-looking friend, and the results showed his moustache and beard to be much cooler than the skin surface. On the other hand, Jesus's moustache and beard, from being drenched with sweat during the Crucifixion, may have held strong concentrations of the developing agent, which would have corrected the coolness.

It is unfortunate that there are so many obstacles to further research. For one thing, Roman Catholic authorities have been reluctant to allow international scientific investigation of the relic. Another snag is the multiplicity of disciplines involved, for any comprehensive investigation will require forensic scientists, fabric experts, chemists and doctors as well as theologians among others.

That we do not know the exact process by which the stains were formed is perhaps not as important as it might be, provided we can be confident that such a natural process can exist and that the conditions governing it are the thermographic and concentration ones mentioned. Once these conditions are assumed, a series of experiments with live bodies could probably establish many more details. New techniques – coating cloth with liquid crystals, for instance – might reveal the exact angle at which the head was bent forward, how much more the left knee was bent than the right, and other small details, as well as a more precise estimate of Jesus's physical dimensions. Also the shape of the ledge, its surface and the position of the hair and supporting pillow could be determined.

In a way, such details would only be supplementing the general theory. The work is necessary, however, to help us to assess the validity of this line of inquiry. Positions become entrenched and convictions rigid in questions of religion, and those of firm faith are often reluctant to leave a sinking island of dogmatic belief. The rewards of arriving at a new and less embattled position, however, can be considerable.

9 A QUESTION OF TIME

It is Sunday morning, and by the sharp light of dawn Mary of Magdala, accompanied by some other women, arrives at the tomb. Thirty-six hours before, they saw the body temporarily wrapped in its Shroud, but not the spices Nicodemus brought to the tomb. Therefore they have now fetched some themselves. They also watched the burial party seal the entrance with a huge stone, and on the way they have been wondering who they can find to roll it back for them. But now the tomb is open, and after the momentary relief that the task is already done they feel terrified by the thought that something may have happened to the body. They run inside and see what Peter and John saw a little later: no body, just two piles of grave-linen.

St John's Gospel is probably the most accurate about what happened next, and he tells us the conclusion Mary drew from the sight. When she had run to the disciples she told them: 'They have taken the Lord out of the tomb, and we do not know where they have laid him' (John 20: 2).

John's deduction from the same visible evidence was, as we saw in the previous chapter, that Jesus had risen. He reached this different conclusion partly because he had not witnessed the burial, so did not know a shroud had been used, and partly because of the positions of the two piles of grave-linen. There was probably one other factor: he suddenly realized that Jesus had foreseen his recovery from death, and that the empty tomb fitted the fulfilment of this prophecy.

Precognition in any form raises fundamental philosophical questions. If man is given free will, it is surely impossible to know, before a choice is made, what it will be. The simplest decision by any one man is likely to spread like a growing wave. The most insignificant and unconsidered action can have repercussions extending to the end of time and history. How therefore can events be foreseen long before they take place? The obvious answer is that since God stands outside the dimension of time, he is able to see the future as well as the past and present; but this answer is not acceptable while man remains bound within the dimension of time, for if God sees the future, He knows the choices we are going to make throughout our lives. Hence our apparent freedom to make a decision when we reach an appropriate point is an illusion. We must run, like a needle in a record groove, down a fixed course, and the meaning and purpose of life has been undermined. We are in this case characters in a puppet play, and God knows all our parts and how the play will end.

Whatever the answer to such paradoxes, the evidence for precognition is extremely strong, and can be seen clearly in parts of the story of Jesus. His own faith in the possibility of accurate prediction was such that he recognized the fate in store for him and accepted it willingly. In fact it happened to him almost exactly as he had foretold it in many respects.

But prophecies are rarely clear, particularly if they are unpleasant. Consult the oracle at Delphi, consider the sayings of many famous visionaries, and it is clear that they had insight into the course events would take. Veiling the message was only sensible, for if recipients are made wise before an event, the event may never take place and the reputations of the prophets will suffer. Any normal person will take avoiding action if warned away from a certain course. He does not accept that this is his fate, as foretold by the Will of God, and go through with it voluntarily. In this respect, of course, Jesus was no normal person. He recognized from the scriptures that, in the role of Messiah, he would be put to death on the Cross and would rise again from the dead after three days, and he warned his disciples that this would happen to him. But again, possibly to prevent their trying to dissuade him from an acceptance of this course of action, he veiled his warning so they did not appreciate it until after the event had happened.

Hence the flash of inspiration John felt when he saw the empty tomb with the grave-linen. 'Destroy this temple,' Jesus had said, 'and in three days I will raise it again.' John continues:

> They said, 'It has taken forty-six years to build this temple. Are you going to raise it again in three days?' But the temple he was speaking of was his body. After his resurrection his disciples recalled what he had said, and they believed the Scripture and the words that Jesus had spoken. [2: 20–22]

At the empty tomb, therefore, the thought 'Christ is risen!' came first to St John, and soon the other disciples believed it as well. Of course this was what he had meant! How blind they had been! All along he had given indications that after three days he would rise again, and this must be the explanation of the empty tomb! He had risen! So the disciples trusted, and the whole Church after them, and in time the weekly gathering of Christians everywhere was fixed for Sunday, the Lord's Day, the day when he walked out of the tomb.

There was only one complication: the tomb had been discovered empty only a day and a half after his death, yet all the prophecies he made had mentioned three days. He had been most specific on this point. It was to be his sign. 'It is a wicked, godless generation that asks for a sign,' he said, 'and the only sign that will be given it is the sign of the prophet Jonah. Jonah was in the sea-monster's belly for three days and three nights, and in the same way the Son of Man will be three days and three nights in the bowels of the earth' (Matthew 12: 39–40). The trial had publicized even further his famous saying that he would rebuild the destroyed temple in three days, and there is the section quoted earlier (page 57) where a guard for the tomb is requested from Pilate: 'We recall how that impostor said while he was still alive, "I am to rise after three days" ' (Matthew 27: 63).

To try to relate these prophecies to the tomb being found empty on the Sunday morning, the disciples started talking about 'the third day'. The second day had started only three hours after his death in that case, for the Jewish day started at sunset, but it was an interpretation that they could accept. The sayings, as recorded, needed to be bent to fit the fact, and it seems remarkable that this was not done with complete consistency. Quite often, perhaps simply in the cause of truth, the form 'in three days' or 'after three days' continued to be used unaltered.

The discrepancy is a stumbling point, though it may seem comparatively unimportant. However, the accuracy of predictions in other aspects of the story is so uncanny that one wonders whether, in this matter of the 'three days', they may not have been equally correct. Admittedly the tomb was empty on the Sunday morning, but then Jesus was still dead by first-century standards and probably in a coma by those of the twentieth. It may not have been till the Monday evening, after the full three days and nights, that he recovered consciousness and returned to life, possibly in the house of Nicodemus.

In this case, for almost two thousand years, the victory has been celebrated slightly too early when, on Easter Sundays everywhere, the bells have rung and Christians have greeted each other with the message that Christ has risen. Nothing should alter this tradition, however, nor is it likely to, for the supposition that Easter Monday was the actual day of the Resurrection could presumably never be proved to everyone's satisfaction.

But there are other discrepancies of time. It has already been pointed out how the Gospels report appearances of Jesus to Mary Magdalene and the Emmaus disciples when, on this theory, the body should still have been in a coma. Can the Gospels, which the Shroud has proved so extraordinarily detailed and accurate in their recording of occurrences, have been far less accurate in the times they give?

The answer is surely yes. They were written neither as histories nor biographies, but to set down the traditional memories of the Church. The order of events is nothing like the same between different Gospels. For instance, in John the cleansing of the Temple comes right at the beginning of the ministry (2: 14–20), while in the Synoptics it is at the end, in Passion Week (Matthew 21: 12–13; Mark 11: 15–19; Luke 19: 45–6). Quite apart from their apparent disregard for the exact times at which less important incidents occurred, so much time elapsed before the Gospels were written down that it would have been almost impossible for the writers to remember precise times. None of the Gospels was probably set down for at least twenty years, though an Aramaic version of St Matthew's Gospel may have been written just within that time. To remember the day of an event, or a sequence of disconnected events, even after a few months is difficult enough, but after two decades this kind of accuracy is virtually impossible, however vividly the pictures of the actions are retained in the memory. Think of a friend, or a distant relation such as a cousin, whom you have not met for quite a long time, and see how certain you can be about the date on which you last saw him.

The recollection of time is distorted by time, and it is highly probable that events not tied exactly to fixed landmarks in the journey of life will shift considerably in the record of the memory. Also, when the originator of a tradition is far removed from the person who writes it down, slight differences occur as it is passed on by each agent, as in the game of Chinese whispers. Cleopas, for instance, may have told the next in line that Jesus met the two of them on the road to Emmaus, 'not long after' the discovery of the empty tomb. He would have remembered it as the first appearance of Jesus to any disciple. Two transmissions of the story could have simply altered the time interval to 'shortly after' and then 'the same day'; particularly when, in their excitement and faith, they would have been concerned to emphasize the marvellous aspects of the story.

There is little doubt, therefore, that statements assigning particular days to sayings and actions unconnected to more epic events are liable to be less accurate. They should not be accepted as strong arguments against the suggested recuperation period.

On the other hand, two factors offer strong support for this suggestion. The first is the interval between the discovery of the empty tomb and the triumphant announcement of the Resurrection in Jerusalem. Luckily, both these events are tied to fixed buoys in the waters of time, the first to the Passover, the second to Pentecost. Thus they could not have floated from their original positions in the years before the Gospels were written. The interval between the two events was clearly seven weeks.

Now if the appearances of Jesus after the Resurrection had begun that Sunday in Jerusalem and on the road to Emmaus, the whole city would have heard about it within a day or two. However, if three or four weeks had been spent in convalescence, and Jesus then went to Galilee by way of Emmaus and Nazareth, most of this interval would be used up. He had still to be with his disciples for a time, and then return near Jerusalem before leaving them, after which they would have walked into the city just about in time for Pentecost. Incidentally, this also explains why Jesus appeared first of all to Cleopas and the other disciple, the more important disciples being in Galilee by then, as well as how his brother James was turned from being no disciple at all into the fervent follower and leader of the Church by the appearance of Jesus in Nazareth.

The second point in favour of this idea is the variety and contradictions contained in the four Gospel accounts of the post-Resurrection appearances. It is only necessary to read them one after the other to see the extraordinary differences; or else to look at a synopsis of the four Gospels, where after the section on the discovery of the tomb the disagreements become so wide that the Gospels have to be considered quite separately.

After the appearance of the man/one angel/two angels to Mary Magdalene and the women, they diverge completely. Matthew gives a very brief paragraph describing the final meeting of the disciples with Jesus. Mark, who ended abruptly with the discovery of the empty tomb in many early copies, has a longer version with Jesus meeting his disciples at table and disappearing from their presence. Luke tells of the meeting on the road to Emmaus, and an appearance among the disciples in Jerusalem before going out to the Ascension. And John, who gives the most information, has the lakeside appearance in Galilee after two appearances in the locked room with the disciples, and the original appearance to Mary Magdalene.

It is all very strange, and the strongest written evidence is perhaps not to be found in the Gospels, but in the first epistle of St Paul to the Corinthians.

First and foremost, I handed on to you the facts which had been imparted to me: that Christ died for our sins, in accordance with the scriptures; that he was buried; and that he was raised to life on the third day, according to the scriptures; and that he appeared to Cephas, and afterwards to the Twelve. Then he appeared to over five hundred of our brothers at once, most of whom are still alive, though some have died. Then he appeared to James, and afterwards to all the apostles. [15: 3–7]

If only the Gospels were straightforward amplifications of Paul's statement! It is also notable that he does not mention the first appearance to Mary Magdalene mentioned in St John's Gospel.

The strange confusion and divergence of the Gospel accounts is much more explicable if we accept a considerable period of recuperation. Imagine the situation in Jerusalem during this period. Everyone knew that the tomb had been discovered empty, and the authorities had been unable to produce the body of Jesus or evidence that it had been stolen. Rumours must have abounded, and the excitement, since it might mean that Jesus had received divine recognition of his Messiahship, must have been widespread. Many in the crowd, remembering his prophecy that if the temple were destroyed he would build it again in three days, must have interpreted this as meaning he would recover from death. Someone perhaps suggested that an angel had carried his body away; or was it two angels? Really? Certainly; the women disciples who discovered the empty tomb on Sunday morning had actually seen them! Someone else said he thought Jesus had cured himself as he did others, so he had been able to walk out of the tomb unaided. What about clothes? I expect he found some; perhaps the gardener left some – the tomb was in a garden, after all – and it was rumoured that the woman disciple, Mary of Magdala, mistook him for a gardener when she first saw him, before he had spoken to her so that she knew it was Jesus.

It was all the stuff from which rumours grow. In this way, during the weeks when Jesus was out of sight, some of them became so fixed that, after two decades, they had acquired the same authenticity as other more accurate reports, and were believed to be categorical truth. It is not to be wondered at, considering the circumstances in which the Gospels were written down, if the message they bore represented a change in the original conception of the nature of Jesus. He was now no longer the 'man, singled out by God' of St Peter's first sermon (Acts 2: 22), but had come to be thought of as the Son of God, the Messiah, who had been raised up from the dead supernaturally by his Father, part of whose nature he shared. Anything that helped to reinforce this impression was emphasized. Small if unintentional distortions in the questions of the times of his appearances, or the suddenness of his appearance or disappearance among his followers, were gradually built into the tradition.

We have still not explained the surprising brevity of the accounts of the post-Resurrection period, but it may be that Jesus had been so changed by his ordeal, not so much physically as mentally, that his power and brilliance were less impressive during his brief latter days with his disciples. We must return to this point later.

10 BEHOLD THE MAN!

The questions of time considered in the previous chapter were examined in the light of the written evidence rather than of a detailed analysis of the stains in the Shroud. The same will be true for the rest of this book. Nevertheless, while the written evidence is the basis of the argument, the light in which it is viewed is completely altered by the three fundamental messages from the Shroud: that the body of Jesus was in a comatose state when it lay in the Shroud; that the body was removed from it before decomposition set in; and that the Gospel accounts of those three days are historically accurate down to some very precise details.

How reassuring this last point seems in an age when biblical criticism has dissected and analysed the Gospel accounts so destructively that one tends to question whether anything in them can be true. But here, from material evidence, we know that, for the Crucifixion at any rate, the descriptions handed on to the Gospel authors were extraordinarily accurate. The reason may be that those particular sections were fragments dictated directly by eyewitnesses, probably by St Peter in the case of St Mark's Gospel and by the Beloved Disciple in the case of St John's.

The Shroud has thus confirmed the accounts of eyewitnesses to an amazing extent. Unfortunately we cannot look to a relic to confirm the words which observers reported they heard, but we should surely accord them a similar respect.

One memory must be true. It is that terrible cry, '*Eli, Eli, lema sabachthani?*', meaning, 'My God, my God, why hast thou forsaken me?' (Mark 15: 34; Matthew 27: 46). It must be true, simply because the only possible motive for recording it must have been its truth. It is similar, in this respect, to the story of St Peter's denial of Christ, which must have remained in his memory like a guilty sore, so that he had to tell others about it and it had to be recorded in the interest of truth, however reluctantly. So with this cry. It had a haunting quality which echoed again in the minds of witnesses whenever they recalled the terrible scene. It was not a case of Jesus quoting the first words of Psalm 22; that would not have been so memorable. 'Jesus cried aloud' – a terrible cry, wrung from the soul of the man – and it resounded in memories over two decades so clearly that the Aramaic form was recorded to add emphasis to that unforgettable call.

Since Jesus almost certainly did call out those words, we must consider what they imply, and the answer is of fundamental importance for judging his nature. He has been pictured as everything from a character in fiction to a live charlatan or an inspired or even perfect man, and on to a part of God in human form at the other extreme. Even Christians of the same denomination have widely differing views here, and it is the nature of Jesus which is the cause of the much greater rifts between the People of the Book: Christians, Jews and Muslims.

What that cry tells us is that, at this moment at least, Jesus was no part of God. If he was completely man at this time, he was presumably completely man throughout his life, though a man 'singled out by God', as St Peter expressed it.

It is extremely difficult to examine such an idea objectively, but we must try to do so. The picture of Jesus in the Synoptic Gospels is of a solid, complete human being, through whom God was able to speak and act in the same way as He could through prophets and saints, but much more effectively. In St John's Gospel, however, the character of Jesus had been raised to being a part of God on earth. It is doubtful whether this has done a service to Christianity, for in many places the Jesus of St John's Gospel seems less relevant as well as less real. The example of the life of Jesus stands unimpaired when, born with far fewer advantages than most of his contemporaries and with no special 'hot line' to God, he lived such a remarkable, effective and valuable life by placing himself entirely at God's service. Plainly he was able to act as an agent of God's words and deeds in this way, but equally plainly God worked through him rather than for his benefit. To Jesus, just as to us, the ways of God were unfathomable, but he had perfect faith in them.

Looked at objectively, the Gospels contain plenty of evidence for Jesus having been not only a normal man of the first century, but also a particularly Jewish one. His knowledge knew very human restraints, and he was strictly first-century Jewish. We see his medical knowledge, therefore, interpreting epilepsy, schizophrenia and other maladies as evil spirits, while his religious ideas at times seem dated and narrow, as when he pictures people going into Heaven with one eye or one foot, having removed the offending member. It is really his powerful Jewishness which argues most forcefully against his being a part of God. He did not see himself as sent to God's creatures in general, but predominantly to his own people. He moved in purely Jewish circles as far as possible, avoiding Sepphoris, Tiberias and other major cities in Israel which had strong Hellenic cultures. His teaching was always within the context of the Jewish religion. He even regarded his life as a sacrifice for the sins of the Jewish people past, present and future, as suggested in Jewish scripture. Had he been part of God, this would have surely been ridiculous, for how could God satisfy Himself for the sins of that one race by sacrificing part of Himself in that way? Jesus' Jewishness shone through his ministry, and at times his description of Gentiles suggested second-class citizens, and though it is true that occasionally he praised the faith he found in a Samaritan or a Roman, his strong preference for Jews lingered among his disciples after his death. It took some time, and a lot of persuasion, before the Jerusalem Church would agree that the message of Jesus was meant for the Gentiles as well as the Jews.

These points would argue for Jesus being a complete, Jewish man, rather than part of the Universal God; but a special one, because he offered himself completely to God's service, entering the role of Messiah for which God had prepared the way.

At the time when Jesus was born all Israel was expecting the arrival of the Messiah, and excitement was intense. For five hundred years God had been silent to His chosen people, but He had indicated through the prophets that His Anointed One would come. The predictions had been obscure, as is usual, and they had been interpreted differently by separate groups of interpreters. There was plenty of scope for variety. Edersheim points out there were 456 passages in the Old Testament which were considered to be Messianic references by the ancient Synagogue. You could make your own selection and form your own picture. Thus we find Messiahs of very different types expected, such as the Branch of Righteousness, the Suffering Servant, and the Son of Man, all relying on particular texts for the basic conceptions.

As for when the Messiah would arrive, the prophecy in Daniel 9 was widely trusted, the seventy weeks being interpreted as 490 years. This meant that the Messiah was due to appear during the reign of Herod (37–4 B.C.), which explains the excitement of the period. However, the Messiah was to be heralded by the Forerunner, as indicated in the last two verses in the Old Testament: 'Look, I will send you the prophet Elijah before the great and terrible day of the Lord comes. He will reconcile fathers to sons and sons to fathers, lest I come and put the land under a ban and destroy it' (Malachi 4: 5–6).

Jesus felt that he was born to fill the role of Messiah so eagerly expected. He must have had an inner conviction from early on that this was why he had been born, and various coincidences and occurrences must have helped to confirm this feeling. For instance, he would have known he was of the House of David, and it was prophesied in Jeremiah 33, Isaiah 11, the Psalms and elsewhere that the Messiah would belong to this line. Then, again, he was born in Bethlehem, an undistinguished if surprising little village, mentioned in Micah 5: 2 thus: 'But you, Bethlehem in Ephrathah, small as you are to be among Judah's clans, out of you shall come forth a governor for Israel.'

It is also possible that his mother told him how she felt his conception to have been an act of God, because at the time she was only engaged to, and had not had intercourse with, her husband. She would have had other strange indications to report to him, such as the visit by the three wise men, who came from a great distance to pay their respects shortly after his birth, prophesying that he would grow up to be a renowned leader.

If it seems hard to accept that Jesus could have accepted his destiny as the Messiah on such evidence, remember that this was the first century, when far more faith was placed in such portents. Moreover, there is a close parallel event recorded in the twentieth century. As a result of meditations and prayers, a party of high-ranking Tibetan monks travelled eastwards from Lhasa in 1935, seeking the reincarnation of the thirteenth Dalai Lama who had died two years previously. Their search led them to Takster, a remote village in the south-east corner of Tibet, and in a small farm with turquoise gables a two-year-old boy proved to be the goal of their quest. Among other signs he recognized and named the disguised lama, picked out items belonging to the previous Dalai Lama, and had certain marks on his body for which the monks were looking. The fourteenth Dalai Lama cannot remember this event, but as a result he grew up to fill the role which, the signs indicated, was meant for him.

In the case of Jesus, strong confirmation that he was the Messiah must have come when he went down to the Jordan to be baptised by John the Baptist. Here was a man who had the outward appearance of Elijah, who had also been connected with the river Jordan. When John prophetically recognized Jesus – and perhaps there was a sudden shaft of sunlight or similar manifestation as Jesus was immersed – his calling was established beyond doubt and his ministry began.

Thus Jesus, the man, knew he was to be the Messiah. What sort of Messiah, though, was he expecting to be? Luckily we know the answer to a certain extent, as Jesus told his disciples. There are three main references where he predicted his fate, and we may study Mark's version in each case as it was probably the source for the other Synoptics' accounts:

Peter replied: 'You are the Messiah.' Then he gave them strict orders not to tell anyone about him; and he began to teach them that the Son of Man had to undergo great sufferings, and to be rejected by the elders, chief priests, and doctors of the law; to be put to death, and to rise again three days afterwards.
[8: 29–31]

Jesus wished it to be kept secret; for he was teaching his disciples, and telling them, 'The Son of Man is now to be given up into the power of men, and they will kill him, and three days after being killed, he will rise again.' But they did not understand what he said and were afraid to ask. [9: 31–2]

He took the Twelve aside and began to tell them what was to happen to him. 'We are now going to Jerusalem,' he said; 'and the Son of Man will be given up to the chief priests and the doctors of the law; they will condemn him to death and hand him over to the foreign power. He will be mocked and spat upon, flogged and killed; and three days afterwards, he will rise again.' [10: 32–4]

The message was simple on each of the three occasions, but the disciples nevertheless had difficulty in understanding it. This was undoubtedly because Jesus's conception of his Messiahship was completely strange to them. It was not the Warrior Messiah whom they were expecting. It was more like the Suffering Servant, foreshadowed clearly in Isaiah 53, and this passage is a most important one, for it was probably the main plank in Jesus's understanding of the role he had to play:

He was despised, he shrank from the sight of men,
tormented and humbled by suffering;
we despised him, we held him of no account,
a thing from which men turn away their eyes.
Yet on himself he bore our sufferings,
our torments he endured,
while we counted him smitten by God,
struck down by disease and misery;
but he was pierced for our transgressions,
tortured for our iniquities;
the chastisement he bore is health for us
and by his scourging we are healed.
We had all strayed like sheep,
each of us had gone his own way:
but the Lord laid upon him
the guilt of us all.

He was afflicted, he submitted to be struck down
and did not open his mouth;
he was led like a sheep to the slaughter,
like a ewe that is dumb before the shearers.
Without protection, without justice, he was taken away;
and who gave a thought to his fate,
how he was cut off from the world of living men,
stricken to the death for my people's transgression?
He was assigned a grave with the wicked,
a burial-place among the refuse of mankind,
though he had done no violence
and spoken no word of treachery.

[Isaiah 53: 3-9]

There were plenty of other references that Jesus may have felt applicable, and judging from his statements to the disciples, he probably used the Psalms a great deal, perhaps feeling that since they were reputedly compiled by David, they were particularly relevant for a descendant. Examples from the Psalms of statements he may have abstracted and joined together, as was done by many at the time, are:

The kings of the earth stand ready, and the rulers conspire together against the Lord and his anointed king. [2: 2]

O God of my praise, be silent no longer, for wicked men heap calumnies upon me. They have lied to my face and ringed me round with words of hate. They have attacked me without a cause, and accused me though I have done nothing unseemly. [109: 1-3]

The stone which the builders rejected has become the chief corner-stone. [118: 22]

Although crucifixion was a most improbable cause of death in Old Testament times, since the Jews used stoning, Zechariah 12: 10 says, 'They shall look on me, on him whom they have pierced'; and Psalm 22: 16 used to include the words, 'They pierced my hands and my feet,' but in the New English Bible this is now rendered as 'They have hacked off my hands and my feet', so the reference to crucifixion is no longer as strong as it was. By the time of Jesus's ministry, however, the Romans were the occupying power, and any sentence of death had to be ratified by them. People were regularly crucified for highway robbery, mutiny, high treason and murder, so Jesus may well have felt that these uncertain hints foretold crucifixion as the most probable method of death. After the event, it is simple to see how parts of Psalms 22 and 69, for instance, predicted some of its details.

It seems, then, that Jesus was expecting to be crucified as a sacrifice for the sins of Israel. He may have expected to die as a result, but certainly not to die on the Cross. In Deuteronomy, the fifth book of Moses, part of the sacred laws of God, it states that a hanged man is accursed in the sight of God (21: 23), and this ruling is also referred to in John 19: 31 and Galatians 3: 13.

Having offered his whole life to God's service, even to the extent of being willing to be crucified, Jesus could feel confident that he would not be cursed in the sight of God. How he was to be saved from dying on the Cross he could not guess, but as Messiah he was to establish the Kingdom of Heaven on earth, and so a divine sign would surely come. He gave his disciples an idea of what would happen:

'The sun will be darkened, the moon will not give her light; the stars will come falling from the sky, the celestial powers will be shaken. Then they will see the Son of Man coming in the clouds with great power and glory, and he will send out the angels and gather his chosen from the four winds, from the farthest bounds of earth to the farthest bounds of heaven . . . I tell you this: the present generation will live to see it all.'
[Mark 13: 24–7, 30]

There was an unnatural darkness at the time of his death on the Cross, but the other manifestations did not occur then; nor when he was with his disciples after the Resurrection, nor after his final departure from them. Yet the disciples were for years afterwards constantly expecting the Son of Man to arrive as in this prophecy, which explains why it was so long before they attempted to write down the words and life of Jesus.

To return to the question of his death, Jesus knew he would not die on the Cross. He would have been fairly sure he would die somehow, but that this would not be the end of the story. There are references to burial in the Psalms and elsewhere, but always of a recovery, or a saving from the corruption of the tomb:

> Therefore my heart exults and my spirit rejoices, my body too rests unafraid; for thou wilt not abandon me to Sheol nor suffer thy faithful servant to see the pit. Thou wilt show me the path of life. [16: 9–11] [Sheol was the Old Testament counterpart of Hades.]

> When the bonds of death held me fast, destructive torrents overtook me, the bonds of Sheol tightened round me, the snares of death were set to catch me; then in anguish of heart I cried to the Lord, I called for help to my God; . . . He reached down from the height and took me, he drew me out of mighty waters, he rescued me from my enemies, strong as they were, from my foes when they grew too powerful for me. [18: 4–6, 16–17]

> But God will ransom my life, he will take me from the power of Sheol. [49: 15]

There are other hopeful passages in the prophets and different Psalms, and even the section in Isaiah 53 depicting the Suffering Servant ends on a hopeful note.

From his analysis, therefore, it seems that Jesus probably concluded he would be saved from extinction by death. He expected it to happen after three days and nights. Such was his faith, he was willing to suffer torture, scourging and crucifixion, confident that a divine sign of Messianic recognition would preserve him.

Hanging in agony on the Cross, three hours after the heavy nails had been slammed through his flesh into the wood, he felt his strength going. There was no chance of his enduring the three days he had expected to hang there. Suddenly it occurred to him that death was coming shortly; the ordeal was too great to bear and he would die on the Cross, accursed in the sight of the God he had trusted. His whole life of service had been wasted, made useless, and his faith had been misplaced. In that awful moment of doubt he gave the most tragic call in history, 'My God, my God, why hast thou forsaken me?' This is surely the implication of his words.

Jesus was a complete man, therefore, and in no way a part of God during his life on earth. This does not necessarily imply that his birth must have been perfectly normal. The Virgin birth story is still feasible, for those who feel that parthenogenesis is necessary to explain the perfection in Jesus. While it has the advantage, by introducing a divine touch to his origin, of adding authority to his words and deeds, there is a concomitant disadvantage. As the proportion of his human nature is lessened, so is his value as an example. He would in this case have been shielded from the difficulties which full humans experience. With no flaw in his nature, he would not have known even the simplest of temptations, such as being naughty when young, so his achievement seems devalued.

'Behold the Man!' said Pilate. It is as a man that Christ is most relevant. True he was the Son of God, and addressed God as Father, but he was also the Son of Man, and made it clear that we are all sons of God. The prayer he taught us to say begins with 'Our Father'. Whether he was a special creation at birth is a matter for personal belief, as is the question of his elevation to being a part of God after ultimate death, and on neither point can the Gospels help us. Their message, together with that of the Shroud, is of his complete humanity when alive, and this matters a great deal.

11 SUPPORTING CAST

There are other recorded words, besides that final cry, which must have been based on truth, if not written down verbatim. One remark which reached the Gospels was made by the centurion, and it is worth considering for what it reveals of his character.

According to Luke, when Jesus died, 'the centurion saw it all, and gave praise to God. "Beyond all doubt", he said, "this man was innocent" ' (23 : 47). In Mark, 'when the centurion who was standing opposite him saw how he died, he said, "Truly this man was a son of God" ' (15 : 39). And in Matthew the centurion as well as his men use the same words.

They are worth quoting, because one of the strongest arguments against Jesus having survived till taken down from the Cross has been the testimony of the Roman soldiers. These men were a hard-hearted, experienced execution party who had probably been chosen because they had taken part in countless crucifixions before, and so there was no chance of their making a mistake. Some have argued that such soldiers were the scum of the earth, and would have had scant regard for the special victim they were killing. Centurions were little better, particularly those given the duty of *exactor mortis*, responsible for remaining with the condemned until they were dead. They were not officers, and it was almost impossible for any of them to rise above their rank. Generally hard, inflexible and insensitive, any natural feelings of

96

compassion had usually been knocked out of them by the gruesome realities of war and such tasks as putting criminals to death.

It is a forceful argument, but in spite of the savage education of their job, some centurions managed to preserve a human touch, a concern for others, throughout their lives. It was a centurion at Capernaum who came to ask Jesus to heal his servant, though he was probably not a Roman since the area was under Herod Antipas. His faith and kindness delighted Jesus. The first Gentile to become a member of the Church was Cornelius, a centurion of the Roman garrison at Caesarea (Acts 10: 1f.). Also Julius, the centurion who escorted St Paul to Rome, was obviously inclined to be friendly towards him (Acts 27: 1 and 43). The centurion at Jesus's crucifixion was therefore not so exceptional in his compassion.

What this argument also fails to take into account is the victim they were executing. True, in a normal crucifixion, they would never make a mistake, but this one was not normal. Who else would have come willingly to this punishment? Others, when their limbs were hammered on to the beams, would have struggled, fought, cried out, or sworn. Jesus did none of these things, as the Prophet had foreseen:

> He was afflicted, he submitted to be struck down
> and did not open his mouth;
> he was led like a sheep to the slaughter,
> like a ewe that is dumb before the shearers.
>
> [Isaiah 53: 7]

Nailed to the Cross, and suffering from the agonizing cramps which were the most painful part of the torture, he had to endure in addition continuous taunting from the passers-by, the chief priests and lawyers. Yet not one word of protest, not one curse, was heard by those at the scene. Even as his strength was failing, he could still think of others, and he told his disciple to look after his mother after he was dead.

If the centurion were at all sensitive, it is no surprise that he was so impressed as to utter the words he did. The soldiers under him were probably not affected, and offering vinegar to Jesus when he said he was thirsty was probably callous cruelty. The passers-by and officials were also unfeeling, and they kept up their cruel mockery. But assuming an effect of compassion on the centurion, we can detect his hand in another section of the story:

> Because it was the eve of Passover, the Jews were anxious that the bodies should not remain on the cross for the coming Sabbath, since that Sabbath was a day of great solemnity; so they requested Pilate to have the legs broken and the bodies taken down. The soldiers accordingly came to the first of his fellow-victims and to the second, and broke their legs; but when they came to Jesus, they found that he was already dead, so they did not break his legs. But one of the soldiers stabbed his side with a lance, and at once there was a flow of blood and water. This is vouched for by an eyewitness, whose evidence is to be trusted. [John 19: 31-5]

The soldiers always smashed the victims' legs and left them hanging for a time to asphyxiate to make sure they were dead. Why did they fail to do this to Jesus? Here, perhaps, we see the preventive hold of the centurion. He had, as *exactor mortis*, to make sure that Jesus was dead, but with his acquired sense of reverence, he may have wanted to disfigure the body as little as possible. He made the soldier pierce the lung, the centre of life, and even then may have ordered restraint so that the soldier gave a gentle jab rather than a vicious thrust. The survival of Jesus may have depended quite largely on the choice of centurion, and the right man had been chosen.

There are other people in the story whom we should reconsider, for this new assessment of the Resurrection and the character of Jesus adds a new dimension to many who were involved. While he was seen as divine or a part of God, the surrounding personalities appear like silhouettes, whether white or black. His supporters are dazzling and unreal in the grace they were afforded – the title 'saint' contributes to this – while anyone who opposed him, or helped in condemning him to death, seems devilishly black. With Jesus seen as a man, the supporting cast become men as well, the new light adding depth to their outline, and we can appreciate them as rounded characters, like ourselves. We can even see how, given the same circumstances, we might have acted as they did. Two whose reputations may have suffered far beyond the range of common sense are Caiaphas and Judas Iscariot, for it is arguable that Caiaphas was an exceptionally wise, adaptable holder of his office, and that Judas was the best and most trustworthy of the disciples.

To take Caiaphas first, we can say at once that he must have had considerable tact and ability. The holding of the post of High Priest was at the discretion of the Roman authorities, and it changed quite frequently. Annas was High Priest from A.D. 7 to 14, and this was described by Josephus as a 'considerable time'. One year saw three successive incumbents. Caiaphus held the post from A.D. 18 to 37 under three procurators.

The exercise of the post must have called for a great deal of intelligence and skill, for, apart from the religious duties, there were heavy political responsibilities. He presided over the Sanhedrin, which was not only the Council of State but also the main civil and ecclesiastical court. He was also the chief official of the Temple, which was an extremely complex and important organization, run by 25,000 men ranging from priests to cleaners, and supported by the enormous income from donations of Jews throughout the Empire. His power, and the burden which went with it, were very great at the best of times.

But the times then were anything but easy, and the greatest political expertise was required. The excitement of the people was continually a grave threat to their safety, for any popular uprising would undoubtedly be crushed with absolute force. The revolt by Simon was within the lifetime of many, and in crushing that Varus had crucified two thousand Jews. Forty years after the death of Jesus, the 'Jewish War' described by Josephus led to the destruction of Jerusalem and the deaths of multitudes of Jews. The dangers were there, and with a tyrant like Pilate as procurator, any sign of revolt would have led to a massacre of the people. The astuteness of Caiaphas must have been partly or mainly responsible for the avoidance of disastrous bloodshed by the Romans during his term of office.

Caiaphas must therefore have been continuously on the watch for trouble. Any local fanatic, and there were always a number, who attracted large crowds was a potential danger, and it would have been unwise and irresponsible of Caiaphas not to have sent priests and agents to investigate and challenge.

While Jesus was attracting multitudes in Galilee, Caiaphas did not worry too much. That was Herod's territory. He apparently arranged for Pharisees to question Jesus and observe him, but nothing more. Had Jesus claimed to be the Messiah openly, it would have been a different matter, but he was careful not to do so and Caiaphas watched and waited.

At last, on his entry into Jerusalem, Jesus gave the sign people had been hoping for. He fulfilled the prophecy:

> Rejoice, rejoice, daughter of Zion,
> shout aloud, daughter of Jerusalem;
> for see, your king is coming to you,
> his cause won, his victory gained,
> humble and mounted on an ass,
> on a foal, the young of a she-ass.
>
> [Zechariah 9: 9]

This was recognized by all the pilgrims, and the joy and excitement were wonderful. The Messiah promised by God had come. 'Hosanna to the Son of David!' they all shouted. 'Blessings on him who comes in the name of the Lord!'

But, from the moment that Jesus had made that claim, Caiaphas had to take action. If Jesus were the Messiah, he should be allowed to occupy the Temple and all there should serve him. But supposing he was a false Messiah. What was Caiaphas to do? He had to do something. If he did nothing, the crowds would swell to proportions which would force the Romans to take action, and this would be disastrous.

To defuse the situation he had to take Jesus away, so he tried to have him arrested in the Temple by daylight; but the crowds around him, and the weakness of the guards, made this impossible. Caiaphas must have been an extremely worried man. It was difficult to see what he could do. Then, absolutely unexpectedly, Judas Iscariot came and offered to lead a party to arrest Jesus at night when there were no people around. Caiaphas and the Inner Council of course accepted.

The point the evangelists fail to make clear is that Caiaphas was acting sensibly, whether Jesus were the Messiah or not.

Obviously if he were false, Caiaphas's line to the Council was correct:

> Thereupon the chief priests and the Pharisees convened a meeting of the Council. 'What action are we taking?' they said. 'This man is performing many signs. If we leave him alone like this the whole populace will believe in him. Then the Romans will come and sweep away our temple and our nation.' But one of them, Caiaphas, who was High Priest that year, said, 'You know nothing whatever; you do not use your judgement; it is more to your interest that one man should die for the people, than that the whole nation should be destroyed.' [John 11: 47–50]

Caiaphas must have been practically certain in his own mind that Jesus was not the Messiah. Apart from anything else, how could the Anointed of God be an illegitimate carpenter, and from Galilee rather than Judea? In any case, the man had broken at least one of the Ten Commandments – that about keeping the Sabbath holy – on several occasions, which was something the true Messiah could not be expected to do.

Apart from being justified if Jesus were not the Messiah, Caiaphas was acting sensibly even if he were. It was his duty to test the man. He knew, as Jesus knew, that the real Messiah could never be 'accursed of God' as described in the fifth book of the sacred law. In getting the Romans to crucify him, Caiaphas was finding the most intelligent way out of his dilemma, for not only would he defuse the situation, he would be testing the truth of Jesus's claim, and he would be demonstrating to Pilate that the Jewish authorities were anxious to suppress any hint of rebellion.

To observe the result of the test, he had to send his observers to the scene, and so we find that, although it was a most holy day, priests were at the unclean place of execution to witness any divine recognition of Messiahship. There 'the chief priests and the doctors of the law jested with one another: "He saved others," they said, "but he cannot save himself. Let the Messiah, the king of Israel, come down from the Cross. If we see that, we shall believe" ' (Mark 15: 31–2).

When the priests reported back that Jesus had died, Caiaphas must have felt very satisfied at the way he had dealt with the situation.

It is true that he had acted illegally the previous night in conducting the cross-examination of Jesus after sunset. Nor was it proper for the judges to question Jesus after the testimony of the witnesses had broken down. And then Caiaphas broke all semblances of legality when, as a last resort, he applied the Oath of the Testimony, 'I adjure thee by the living God . . .' (Matthew 26: 63) to force an admission from Jesus. Yet, putting ourselves in Caiaphas's position, he simply had to convict Jesus somehow. To have released him, admitting the arrest was unsuccessful, would have raised the popular appeal of Jesus to a frenzy that would have quickly led to an uprising and genocide. What Caiaphas did was empirically sound, if illegal, and in his eyes he had no option, and the ends justified the means.

The other person who deserves a kinder view is Judas Iscariot. In the role in which he appears in the Gospels he is a complete enigma. If man has free will to choose what he does with his life, it is impossible to conceive a creature of God's being born to do what he did, for he was compelled to carry out the worst betrayal in history.

In his circumstances, his action is inexplicable under the conventional interpretation. How could anyone have been a disciple of Jesus for two years or so, and then betray him for a small sum of money so that he was put to death? It is ridiculous. And would Jesus have chosen a man with such a flaw in his character as an apostle? Jesus 'knew men so well, all of them, that he needed no evidence from others about a man, for he himself could tell what was in a man' (John 2: 24–5). He could recognize a devil in a stranger at sight, and expel it. Would he have allowed one to enter one of his chosen followers and have done nothing about it?

We do not know the biographical details of Judas: simply that he was the son of Simon Iscariot (John 6: 71). The fact that father and son had the same name indicates that it almost certainly meant 'of Kerioth', a village in Judea. The other eleven disciples came from Galilee, which could so easily have led to friction, and it is remarkable that there is no suggestion of a rift between them during the ministry. It is also surprising that, when they felt certain he had been guilty of betraying their beloved Master, his disciples suspect him of only one earlier crime: that of pilfering the money box (John 12: 446). There is no other derogatory reference, so he must have been a remarkable man. It is also worth mentioning that, while the other disciples suggest he betrayed Jesus because a devil suddenly entered him, he was given the power to cast out devils with the others earlier in the ministry, and presumably he exercised it successfully or it would have been reported otherwise.

To understand Judas's actions, we need to go back to Jesus's predictions of his fate. It is clear that he explained to his disciples on at least three occasions his interpretation of the scriptures: that he would be condemned to death by the authorities, and be sacrificed for the sins of Israel. The Gospels imply that his disciples could not accept, or refused to accept, that this was his concept of Messiahship, and Peter 'took him by the arm and began to rebuke him: "Heaven forbid!" he said. "No, Lord, this shall never happen to you." Then Jesus turned and said to Peter, "Away with you, Satan; you are a stumbling-block to me. You think as men think, not as God thinks" ' (Matthew 16: 22–3).

The only disciple who was probably capable of understanding Jesus's thoughts on this was Judas. He was from quite a different background from the others, and would have had the strict religious education of a Judean child. First they were allowed into the community with the act of circumcision, and in childhood in the home would have learnt much about religion from the observed feasts, customs and prayers. They were regularly instructed in texts of the Scripture containing the same letters as their Hebrew names, and had to memorize some Psalms. Schools were compulsory from the age of five or six, and after learning to read and write they studied the Holy Scriptures exclusively, starting with Leviticus, then the rest of the Pentateuch, followed by the Prophets and other books. In the harsh, barren environment of Judea, Judas would have had a much more formal and extensive education than the others in the lush, easy-going area around the Sea of Galilee.

Jesus, obviously, was extremely well-versed in the Scriptures, and it is quite possible that the only disciple capable of discussing the prophecies and the role of the Messiah with him in detail was

Judas. He, then, may have been the only one who understood, and who was persuaded to agree with, Jesus's conclusions, the others not having the learning to do so.

Jesus arrived in Jerusalem hoping, and expecting, to be arrested once he had given the sign that he was the Messiah. The authorities would have wanted to arrest him, but the presence of the sympathetic crowds made it extremely difficult for the authorities to do so without causing the riot they aimed to avoid. A go-between was needed, and the obvious disciple for Jesus to choose was Judas. Apart from being the only one to see the reason for the arrest, he would have been most familiar with Jerusalem and better able, with his Judean speech and education, to make the right contacts.

The next question was one of timing. Jesus, we know, wanted to have the Passover Meal with his disciples before being handed over, and he expected to die as the sheep were being sacrificed in the Temple for the Passover meal on the Friday. The two successive days of Passover meals seem puzzling, but the number of Jews in Jerusalem for the festival was enormous, and they had to eat their meal after dark in the area of Greater Jerusalem. This included Bethphage and the Mount of Olives, but not Bethany, and although the hillsides were covered with tents and the houses inside the city walls let visitors use their spare rooms, the accommodation was probably insufficient. Because of this, and the problem of sacrificing the very great number of animals in the Temple in preparation, it seems that two days were allowed for it. There was also, probably, a difference in the Galilean calendar, which meant that the Passover was for them celebrated a day early. We can presume that many of the visitors from abroad and Galilee sacrificed their animals and ate their meals on the Thursday, leaving the accommodation they had occupied for Judeans and stricter Jews to use on the Friday. This may also explain why the ecstatic crowd who acclaimed Jesus on his entry into Jerusalem at the beginning of the week was not there to support him outside the Antonia on the Friday morning. The rigid, prim Judeans were more easily swayed by Caiaphas's agents to demand the crucifixion of Jesus.

If this interpretation is correct, Jesus would have agreed with Judas that the arrest should take place on the Thursday night.

We know that Judas made a preliminary visit to warn the council. 'Then Judas Iscariot, one of the Twelve, went to the chief priests to betray him to them. When they heard what he had come for, they were greatly pleased, and promised him money' (Mark 14: 10–11). The thirty pieces of silver was not much. As a recompense for betrayal of a beloved master, it was plainly ridiculous, and the council may have insisted on Judas taking it as it was the advertised reward, or as a deliberate insult, as it was the fine payable for the death of a slave.

The meeting-place he suggested was an easily recognized one. The Garden of Gethsemane was a cypress and olive grove, with a large olive press in it, opposite the walls of Jerusalem across the Kidron Valley. The hillsides around would have been covered with the tents of visitors to the festival, but the walled garden itself would have been a quiet meeting-place. After suggesting this to the priests, and promising to come to take the arresting party to the spot, Judas would have rejoined the disciples and Jesus.

It appears that the timing went wrong on the Thursday evening. First, the Passover meal may have taken longer than anticipated, so that Judas had to leave before it was over to contact the arresting party. Jesus made a final attempt to warn the others what was going to happen:

> After saying this, Jesus exclaimed in deep agitation of spirit, 'In truth, in very truth I tell you, one of you is going to betray me.' The disciples looked at one another in bewilderment: whom could he be speaking of? One of them, the disciple he loved, was reclining close beside Jesus. So Simon Peter nodded to him and said, 'Ask who it is he means.' That disciple, as he reclined, leaned back close to Jesus and asked, 'Lord, who is it?' Jesus replied, 'It is the man to whom I give this piece of bread when I have dipped it in the dish.' Then, after dipping it in the dish, he took it out and gave it to Judas son of Simon Iscariot. As soon as Judas had received it Satan entered him. Jesus said to him, 'Do quickly what you have to do.' No one at the table understood what he meant by this. Some supposed that, as Judas was in charge of the common purse, Jesus was telling him to buy what was needed for the festival, or to make some

gift to the poor. Judas, then, received the bread and went out. It was night. [John 13 : 21–30]

There was no doubt from this that Jesus knew what Judas was about to do. It was prearranged. Judas was doing what Jesus had asked him to do. This is confirmed by the extraordinarily long wait in the Garden of Gethsemane. The disciples fell asleep three times, such was the delay, and they must have wondered why they could not return to their tents and their beds. But Jesus could not leave. He had promised Judas he would be there.

Why the party took so long to come to arrest him we cannot tell. It may be that Caiaphas went to Pilate to warn him that a man charged with treason would need rapid ratification of the death sentence in the morning, and Pilate delayed him. Perhaps the Romans insisted on some of their troops being present, and they had to get ready. In any case, the delay must have exasperated Judas, knowing the agony of mind Jesus must be suffering. Eventually it was over, and the unnecessarily large party – a crowd including soldiers, police from the chief priests and Pharisees – set out. It crossed the Kidron, plainly visible from the Garden of Gethsemane, and Jesus waited for them.

When they reached the Garden, Judas was at the front, 'and stepping forward at once, he said "Hail, Rabbi!" and kissed him. Jesus replied, "Friend, do what you are here to do." They then came forward, seized Jesus, and held him fast' (Matthew 26: 49–50).

That embrace is another important point. It was quite obvious which person was Jesus, and in fact in St John's Gospel he tells the arresting party as it comes up that he is the man they are looking for. The disciples, thinking back after the death of Jesus, convinced that Judas had betrayed him for devilish reasons, could only explain that kiss as a sign of recognition for the soldiers. Personally I think it was much more likely a token of thanks and friendship, for Judas had accomplished a difficult task, perhaps unwillingly as a result of persuasion from Jesus.

Judas's mission was accomplished, and as the drama approaches its climax, the spotlight stays on Jesus, and we only glimpse Judas briefly again at his death.

There are two accounts of this, in Matthew 21 and Acts 1.

Comparing them shows how variations occurred in the traditions before they were set down. In Matthew, Judas returned the money to the chief priests and elders, who bought the Potters' Field with it, its name being changed to Blood Acre since it was bought with the price of blood. Then Judas hanged himself. In Acts, Judas kept the money and bought the field with it himself, but, and the description does not necessarily imply suicide, 'he fell forward on the ground, and burst open, so that his entrails poured out'. The term 'Blood Acre' referred to his own blood in this case.

The variations are wide, but certain points are reasonably consistent. The field must have been associated with the reward paid to Judas, and he must have died by suicide or accident not long after Jesus's arrest. It is surprising we cannot be sure how he died, but by then he played a minor part. Assuming Judas to have acted in Jesus's interest by bringing about the arrest, however, we can try to put ourselves in his position to guess at what really happened to him.

He had done as Jesus had asked him to do, that Thursday night, and Jesus had shown his gratitude. Now he could only wait, tormented by the thought of what Jesus was suffering. The night would have passed slowly, and he could imagine Jesus in the High Priest's house, from which he had been barred on return with the arresting party. It was no laughing matter, being held by members of the guard there; they liked nothing better than kicking a man when he was down. Throughout the night Judas still prayed and suffered. He wanted to try to share the ordeal of his friend and Master to the greatest extent he could.

Eventually the silver trumpets from the Temple would have sounded over the city to announce the dawn, and people should have started moving around. Perhaps he needed air by then, and decided to roam the streets, losing himself in the crowds.

What he did for much of the day we cannot tell. He may possibly have been with the crowd at the foot of the Antonia steps when Jesus was interrogated by Pilate. Almost certainly he was not a witness of the Crucifixion, for his presence would have been recorded, and he should have guessed how the other disciples might have misinterpreted his action in arranging the arrest. He would have had to question others to find out what was happening. When told that Jesus had been sentenced to crucifixion, and during the time it was being carried out, his sense of horror at what Jesus must be suffering would have been sweetened very slightly by the thought that, quite remarkably, everything was happening as Jesus had foretold. Throughout the long, close afternoon, he would have imagined what his Master was suffering only too accurately, for the sight of the naked, twisting bodies, pressing up on their feet for breath, and crying out in agony from the cramps they endured, was all too common. The execution sites were always near to the ways where people pass, to act as a deterrent, so all knew it to be the cruellest death possible. And this torture Jesus was expecting to survive three days! Three days and three nights, in fact, until the Messianic sign was given him, and perhaps the Kingdom of God inaugurated on earth.

It became very dark, and there was a strong earth tremor. As the afternoon passed, Judas must have heard the first rumour that Jesus had died. Desperately he would have rushed around for other witnesses. Surely it could not be true? How could Jesus have died? How could he be cursed of God?

But confirmation came. Witness after witness had seen his body, slumped, distorted, motionless on the Cross for hours with no sign of breath.

Then would have come the terrible realization. What had he done? What *had* he done? Through his agency the best man who ever lived, the greatest of the Prophets, the finest friend, the truest Master, had been cruelly executed by the authorities. It had been his, Judas's, fault. He should never have agreed to it.

Full of disgust, fury and horror, he seized the bag of coins and stormed to the Sanhedrin by the Temple Gate. There the chief priests were sitting, hearing the report of the representatives who had witnessed Jesus's death, with no Messianic sign apparently granted. Yelling his fury and abhorrence, he would have flung down the coins on the floor in front of them and run out. Unable to live with his conscience a moment longer, he would have left and committed suicide shortly after.

This account of his character and actions seems to fit the facts so much better than the traditional view. If it is true, it is easy to see how the other disciples mistook his motives and regarded him as the worst traitor in history. He had seemed such a wonderful person when they first knew him, and Jesus had appeared to hold him in a higher regard than any of them. So clever, too; and cheerful and honest. How could he have done it? He had never shown any sign at all of being untrustworthy. He was in charge of the money throughout the ministry, so perhaps he may have taken a little of that sometimes without anyone knowing. There were no other symptoms ever. It must have been a devil entering him suddenly; that was the only possible explanation.

Poor Judas! The finest disciple of the best man who ever lived, and because he acted as his Master wanted him to, his name has been anathema for almost two thousand years.

12 THE RISEN CHRIST

Monday evening, and perhaps, in the shelter of Nicodemus's house, the body of Jesus started to breathe properly again; life, as they defined it, had returned. Slowly he recovered consciousness, full of pain, to find Joseph or Nicodemus watching over him. He would have wondered where he was and what had happened.

We need to try to imagine how things would have appeared to him, remembering that he had the beliefs of the first century. I emphasize this, because it would be absolutely wrong to suggest that, since he had recovered from a comatose state and had not really died by twentieth-century standards, Jesus was a hoax. This would be nonsense.

As he came round, and asked whoever was tending him where he was, he would have been told how he had died on the Cross. He would have believed it as much as his informants did.

Obviously, for a present-day reader, this is difficult to appreciate, but to me it is entirely credible. I once encountered a case which was far more bizarre: a man, told he was dead by his friends as he came round from nearly drowning, believed that he was in fact dead, as did his friends, for the rest of his life. It is worth giving an account of this incident as it may throw light on the conviction of Jesus and his disciples that he had recovered from being absolutely dead.

In 1945 I was serving with the 1st King George V's Own Gurkha Rifles, and was posted from the Regimental Centre at

Dharmsala, now the home of the Dalai Lama, to the First Battalion (1/1 GR) at Nagpur. Churamanni Rana, the dead man of the story, had belonged to the battalion until a few months before I arrived, so I heard about him from the other officers in the Mess, most of whom had come across him. The tale had always fascinated me, and as it seemed relevant to my research into the Shroud, I wrote to Col John Rennie who had been the officer mainly involved. I did not want to give what I remembered being told, since mine was second-hand evidence, and I was afraid my imagination might have embellished details over the years. Here is his reply:

'Chronologically things took place somehow like this:
1/1 GR was doing some jungle warfare training in the jungles of S. India in the vicinity of Bangalore. While on a company training test in a river crossing I was suddenly aroused by shouts of "Manchhe dubyo" – "A man has gone under." We had constructed bamboo rafts which were pulled back and forth across the river to ferry the heavy equipment across. Non-swimmers were told to hang on to the rafts to cross over. Churamanni Rana, one of C Company's smaller and less thought of Riflemen, had for some unknown reason let go mid stream and sunk like a stone. The current was fairly swift at that point and the river about 15 feet deep. I went in after him and due to the murky water had to dive many times before I located him. Finally I wrapped my legs around him and swam to the surface. It must have been at least ten minutes after he sank until we got him ashore. Luckily I had a fairly good knowledge of life-saving and started artificial respiration on him. After about ten minutes he started breathing. The men were astounded. They had been saying, "Leave him alone, sahib; he is dead" all the time I was working on him.

After a while when I had pumped all the water I could out of him he threw up, then sat up and stared around. The whites of his eyes had turned bright red. I sent him to the Battalion 1st Aid Station and pretty well forgot about the whole thing.

After we returned to the base camp some days later, I was standing by myself in the jungle when suddenly Churamanni appeared and said to me that he was really dead and that all his belongings were now mine; his wife and child and cow and so forth.

I then noticed the other men never spoke to him directly and always used the past tense when mentioning him.

A few months later, during one of our earlier skirmishes in Burma, when the firing subsided I asked what casualties we had and was told two men killed. Later in the day I passed a detail pushing a captured Jap hand-cart down the road with a blanket over it. I asked what was under the blanket, and was told it was the two casualties from the skirmish. I pulled the blanket back and saw three bodies, and asked them about it and was told – "Oh that one is Churamanni but we didn't count him because he was drowned in the river crossing a few months ago."

That's about it! I don't recall anything about sticking pins in the man, but after the river crossing he acted as though he was a zombie and never spoke a word except his brief announcement of his "will" to me.

I have no explanation of the other men's attitude towards him. I am sure they had never seen artificial respiration dramatically demonstrated before, and they probably couldn't really accept it as a fact. Drowning is a fairly common death among Gurkhas in their natural habitat . . .'

That is the story. The reference to 'sticking pins in the man' is because, in my letter to him, I mentioned I had heard from one of the other officers that Churamanni was so sure he was dead, he was insensitive to pain, and you could stick pins right through his flesh.

John Rennie was awarded a medal for the rescue, and the citation reads: ' . . . which is hereby awarded him for having, on the 7th of January, 1945, gone to the rescue of a man who was in imminent danger of drowning in the Bhadra River, Balehonnur, Southern India, and whose life he gallantly saved'.

There are two points from this story which are worth considering in the case of Jesus. The first is obvious: if a large body of men in the twentieth century could be sure that their friend walking around with them was dead, and the man believed it too, how much more likely is it that the people to whom Jesus appeared could have assumed he had been completely dead and become alive again? And that *he* should have believed it, too.

The second point worries me. Churamanni was obviously affected by his experience mentally, so that he behaved like a zombie. While Jesus's body hung on the Cross in a comatose state, his heart would have been barely beating and the fluid in his body would have drained to his legs. His brain may therefore have been so starved of oxygen that some permanent damage resulted. I am not suggesting he became a zombie, for he was able to find his way around and talk rationally to those he met. There may, however, have been some damage. Physically he would have recovered almost perfectly, though the terrible suffering may have altered his appearance; people's looks can change considerably during an extreme illness. It may be that his mental powers suffered to a certain extent, so that he was unable to resume his ministry forcefully, and also that his strange state may explain the odd, unsatisfactory accounts of his post-Resurrection appearances.

The evidence of his presence, however, and his consequent miraculous defeat of death were sufficient to transform the disciples.

To go deeper into the subject of those appearances is like sailing into a stretch of sea with the aid of several charts which agree in hardly any details. We can presume that after leaving Jerusalem he went west, and the first of his disciples he met were Cleopas and his friend on the road to Emmaus. It is in no way surprising they did not recognize him, for, apart from altered looks, the possibility that Jesus could appear again four weeks after his death would not have occurred to them.

His journey then probably turned north, along the high route to Galilee, and he may have visited his family at Nazareth. He would have wanted to comfort his mother, whom he had last seen from the Cross, but in fact she would not have been there (John 19: 27), only the other members of his family, including James. During his ministry there seems to have been a cold indifference from his family, and none apparently became a disciple. Then, soon after the Church was founded, James is plainly a keen supporter and indeed becomes leader, dying for its cause years later. Since James would not have been on the Sea of Galilee with the other disciples, it is probable that Jesus went to the family home, and that his defeat of the bonds of death converted James to his support.

So to the lake, where his dispirited, unhappy disciples were attempting to return to their earlier occupations. 'Strike the shepherd, and the sheep will be scattered,' Zechariah had prophesied, but he who was known as the Good Shepherd had returned to bring them together again.

Their joy can be imagined, and of that joy, and the conviction that he had triumphed and had Messianic recognition, the Church was born. There was no hoax; Jesus was also sure he had died. No doubt they asked him about his recovery, and he would have kept silent about the shelter afforded him by Joseph of Arimathea and Nicodemus so as not to add to their danger. Noncommittal replies would then have been sensible and necessary, and only in the years after he had left them, as increasing elements of divinity were added to his character by St Paul and St John, would those vague answers be taken as evidence of the supernatural aspects of his recovery.

He did not stay with them long. Even St John's Gospel, which has the longest report, mentions only three appearances to his disciples. How he left them is not clear. In Luke 'he led them out as far as Bethany, and blessed them with uplifted hands; and in the act of blessing he parted from them' (24: 50–51). In the extended Mark, he appeared to the eleven at table and, 'after talking with them the Lord Jesus was taken up into heaven, and he took his seat at the right hand of God' (16: 19). Neither John or Matthew describes the parting.

With no supernatural intervention up to this point, one would expect Jesus simply to have left them, walking away, perhaps into a cloud on the mountainside. And then what? The authorities never found him, and they must have been searching from the moment rumours started that he had left the tomb. If he lived on, it must have been out of reach of Jerusalem. Perhaps he went as the returned Teacher of Righteousness so eagerly awaited by the Essene community by the Dead Sea. He may even have gone abroad, and there are traditions that he visited places as wide apart as North America and Pakistan.

Much more likely is that he died soon afterwards. Beyond the limits of the material universe is a mystery to us, but it is possible that during the three days after crucifixion he may well have had some experience of the God he had served, so that a return to this life was a burden, and as soon as his task was completed he may have longed to be rid of his body. In that case he may have lost the will to live and have died soon afterwards.

There is one nagging doubt to prevent this solution from being satisfactory. The section in Isaiah which prophesied the plight of the Suffering Servant does not end with death. It continues thus:

> He was assigned a grave with the wicked,
> a burial-place among the refuse of mankind,
> though he had done no violence
> and spoken no word of treachery.
> Yet the Lord took thought for his tortured servant
> And healed him who had made himself a sacrifice for sin,
> so shall he enjoy long life and see his children's children.
>
> [Isaiah 53: 9–10]

Could Jesus have married and settled down to live in obscurity? Perhaps. But at that stage does it matter? He was no longer the channel for the words of God, and we cannot learn from his example. His work was done, and what happened to his body is of relatively little importance. What is significant is his, and God's, spiritual promise from the end of St Matthew's Gospel: 'Be assured, I am with you always, to the end of time.'

13 THE MESSAGE

For many Christians the supernatural element in the New Testament accounts of the Resurrection provides a prop for their faith, and there is a heavy responsibility attached to saying anything that may damage this. I can only hope that any new concept of Jesus's role which emerges from a study of the Shroud will provide an alternative, stronger support. Certainly, for a great number of people, this same supernatural element has stretched their credulity beyond its limits, and their inability to believe this one part of the package has led them to reject the whole.

That is the trouble with having packages. It is the full formulation of the tenets of the Church, the assembly of dogmas, the writing of creeds, that has led to the fragmentation of the Christian religion. It is difficult to argue against the items in an unwritten constitution, but as soon as a creed of belief is set down in detail, parts of it must give offence or raise conscientious issues.

Look, for instance, at the Old Roman Creed, the first in the Christian Church, set down in about A.D. 100 and based on the teaching of Peter and Paul:

I   1 I believe in God, Father Almighty;
II 2 And in Christ Jesus, His only Son, our Lord,
    3 Who was born of the Holy Ghost and the Virgin Mary,
    4 crucified under Pontius Pilate and buried,

5 the third day He rose from the dead,

6 He ascended into heaven,

7 sitteth at the right hand of the Father,

8 thence He shall come to judge living and dead.

III 9 And in the Holy Ghost,

10 Holy Church,

11 remission of sins,

12 resurrection of the flesh.

Already the points for dissension are obvious, and this is the simplest and earliest of the creeds. There are plenty of ministers in the Church today, for instance, who are conscientiously unable to accept parts of it. The most obvious causes for disbelief are probably 'His only Son', 'Born of the Holy Ghost and the Virgin Mary', the 'remission of sins' and the 'resurrection of the flesh', but there are others.

Jesus did not give his disciples a creed. Perhaps he realized the dangers of doing so. Belief is a very personal thing. It is creeds which create the points of difference which cause sects to break away from the central body of belief. Instead of looking for the common foundation, they have cherished their specific small preserves, fighting against those whose beliefs are not quite the same, and trying to impose their own creeds on others, often in place of far more suitable, local traditions. In the name of Jesus, bloody crusades have been fought and highly developed civilizations, such as that of the Incas, destroyed, while the fierce animosity between different brands of Christianity has led to civil wars and feuds in utter antithesis to the basic message of their joint founder. Today we see the unhappy example of Ulster.

To find the common core of belief in all Christians is not easy, but one can surely say that all believe that Jesus lived, died, and rose again from the dead – all those points of which the Holy Shroud is proof positive.

It is the question of the nature of Jesus which has caused so much division. Was he God incarnate, an aspect of God, or man? Is God Three Persons or One? Such debates not only separate Christians from each other, but have placed a great gulf between them and the Jews and all the world's other religions.

That Jesus was a complete man on earth seems to me to be the vital message of the Shroud, and it is a message that can reunite

Christians and all the other sons of God. Some Christians may also happen to believe that his birth was special in some way – perhaps a case of parthenogenesis – and that after death his achievement was acknowledged and rewarded by an especial absorption into God, but while on earth he was a complete human, with no specific advantages over others. If the Shroud's message is accepted in this light, many old wounds could be healed. For instance, at present the Jews are still often considered by Christians to be the race which killed the Son of God. Killing a man is nothing like so culpable, and I have tried to show how, in fact, the actions of Caiaphas, Judas Iscariot and the other Jews were not only understandable but sensible, and in Judas's case positively creditable. But the Shroud also shows that Jesus did in fact receive the Messianic recognition he sought, and this must put Christians in a different light with the Jews. Likewise Muslims, who believe Jesus to have been a great prophet of God, will no longer need to be offended by dogmatic Christian insistence on his divinity.

Belief that Jesus was no more than a man when on earth does not, in my view, prevent one being a Christian. It is because he was a complete human that his example is so important, for this means that he really did suffer the temptations which affect us all, and also shared our doubts. As a physical body motivated by part of God, unable even to get up to mischief when a child, he must be far less relevant to our needs and predicaments.

Many Christian churches, however, would not accept a thesis of Christ's total humanity, and the question arises of whether one should continue to attend church services if individual items of dogma no longer seem acceptable. Personally, I do not think that this should be a hindrance. Faith is a very personal possession, and any congregation is bound to contain a wide range of beliefs. Worship is helped by the environment and the company, and the exact wording of the service need not be analysed sentence by sentence but enjoyed as a whole, like a Shakespeare play. The priest who is officiating does not in all probability believe without reservation every word of the creed which is the foundation of the service, and the same would apply to most members of the congregation in one way or another. Surely anyone who claims to be a practising Christian should find the church and the service that suits him best, and then attend regularly. Dr Johnson had some wise words on the subject:

> To be of no church is dangerous. Religion, of which the rewards are distant, and which is animated only by Faith and Hope, will glide by degrees out of the mind, unless it be invigorated and reimpressed by external ordinances, by stated calls to worship, and the salutary influence of example.

To reduce Jesus to a complete human from being a part of God on earth, and show that there is a rational explanation for the Resurrection, is not to remove the spiritual element from the story. Showing that material laws were not broken no more eliminates the divine touches than the laws of refraction remove the beauty from colours. The prophecies, the characters involved, the formation and preservation of the stains in the Shroud, the whole wonderful story show a sense of divine concentration on that one event that haphazard conjunctions or statistical chances cannot explain. There is a spiritual as well as a material field at work, influencing the proceedings. How such powers operate we cannot tell, but from observed evidence, from the miracles at Lourdes and elsewhere, from the behaviour of animals and plants, from a whole range of phenomena beyond the range of the physical laws known to us at present, there is a field through which the force of faith can bend, stop or even reverse material processes, and it is on this plane that God operates.

The spiritual field is as much an aspect of nature as the material one, and the two interact. In natural science we have tended to study only the material laws, and to construct a rational edifice we have studied them in conditions which as far as possible exclude the spiritual element. In the cool, clinical atmosphere of a laboratory, experiments can be observed and repeated with the same result time after time. The essential condition, 'provided no spiritual interference is present', is taken for granted. Once those same laws are taken outside, where faith can play a part, they can no longer predict what will happen. To take a simple case, in the laboratory one can observe the changes which take place in skin tissue when it is heated, yet no alteration takes place to the soles of the feet of the ecstatic tribesmen who walk across red-hot coals in religious ceremonies. The less the people concerned are indoctrinated with a trust in materialism, the less such processes can be predicted.

The spiritual side of nature no doubt also has its laws, and these presumably act predictably when there is no material interference. To investigate them is difficult, and I suspect that applying the methods devised for investigating material processes will never reveal much of importance, for the process of measurement designed to stop outside interference must reduce or eliminate the subject being studied. There must be a fundamental limit at the material–spirit 'interface' similar to Heisenberg's Uncertainty Principle.

For those unfamiliar with this fundamental hypothesis, it is a mathematical expression of the limit of the knowledge we can obtain. It is impossible to push knowledge further, because the act of measuring interferes with what we are trying to measure. It applies, for instance, at the wave–particle interface of the electron. If you consider the electron as a particle, and devise an experiment to determine exactly where it is, you cannot – it is a physical impossibility – measure its velocity, hence its momentum, hence its wavelength (its essential wave quality) all at the same time. If, treating the electron as a wave, you measure its wavelength, you inevitably have a long train of a wave, so cannot tell where it is exactly as a particle. Yet scientists are quite happy to believe that electrons exist, but demand stricter proofs for spiritual phenomena.

Attempts are being made to tie down such effects as telepathy, precognition and clairvoyance with a statistical and clinical certainty, but the laboratory approach developed for material science is the worst possible method. There is plenty of evidence to suggest that, as man became more civilized, developing verbal communication and material expertise, he lost many of the spiritual attributes of his ancestors. Primitive tribes in Africa and Asia live, even now, in harmony with the spiritual world, so that telepathy, 'miraculous' cures, precognition and many other effects rarely seen in the Western world are for them quite commonplace, and this is where the investigations should begin. These people, too, have natural religions, not because they need to have a god, but because they are more aware of God.

The application of a modified Uncertainty Principle may well mean that the ultimate question, 'Does God exist?' can never be satisfactorily proved by scientific methods. God is a Spirit, so we need to cultivate the spiritual awareness of primitive tribes and holy men in the East. Perhaps this attribute could be trained and developed, instead of repressed, in the children of the future.

Such awareness was common coin among the contemporaries of Jesus. The power of the spirit over the body was generally recognized, and this belief gave an atmosphere in which instantaneous cures, miraculous by our standards, would have been far more easily accomplished. It has also been said that the haloes around the heads of saints in early paintings show how people were then able to perceive the spiritual aura possessed by every man.

The acceptance of the existence of God is a matter of faith, but in an age when our spiritual perception is weak, the material evidence of the Shroud becomes of the utmost importance. It is not just that from it we know that Jesus lived, died and rose again. His almost unbelievable selflessness is undeniably recorded. We have confirmation, too, that the reports of his suffering were correct down to fine details, and that the written accounts are remarkably reliable. From this material evidence we can therefore be certain that Jesus trusted the God he served to such an extent that he was willing to sacrifice himself to crucifixion, trusting in God's promise, through the prophets, that he would not suffer the corruption of death. The Shroud's material proof that he was in reality saved in such a remarkable way is the strongest possible evidence for the existence of the God which Jesus shared with us.

The linen strip with its stains was, I believe, preserved for the twentieth century. Its authenticity and its message awaited the use of photography as the century began. It is material evidence for those who, rendered insensitive to the spiritual world by technological development, distrust anything which cannot be demonstrated from substantial, observable evidence. Through it millions may regain faith, and never was it more urgently needed. Consider the situation to which our worldly goods and aspirations have led us. In spite of the great advances in comfort, convenience and material provision, man is as violent and selfish as he ever was, while science has placed in his hands tools that could lead to total destruction. Technology has continued to accelerate like a newly formed avalanche, and there seems to be no way of stopping its potentially annihilating progress. Or no material way. We need a faith that will move mountains, and more and more people are looking to religion to provide an answer. The Shroud could help in this. Its purpose is to unify, not to divide; to confirm a new faith rather than to knock an old one.

A single person, ex-King Umberto II of Savoy, is the owner of the relic, and he has assigned custodianship to the Roman Catholic Church. Up to now the Church authorities have, so to speak, guarded it religiously. The general public has not been allowed to view it, except on television, since 1933, and requests from scientists of international repute and many denominations to examine it have been refused. A commission of experts, carefully selected, investigated it from 1969 onwards, but the constitution of the committee, the methods of research employed, and the limited objectives were all inadequate.

Now there are signs at last of a more constructive approach. This year, 1978, to coincide with the 400th anniversary of the arrival of the relic in the city, Turin is staging an international conference. Also the relic will be on public display for the whole of September. The Holy Shroud Guild in the USA has assembled an extremely able team of scientists who are ready to examine the Shroud scientifically by the most up-to-date methods, and a request for this research to be conducted to coincide with the conference has been sympathetically received. Several new techniques would be involved, mainly using different wavelengths across a wide section of the electromagnetic spectrum. No damage can be done, but knowledge is bound to be extended, and there is the hope that valuable clues to the process by which the image was in the first place formed on the cloth may be among the discoveries.

What message the Shroud will convey through this or any future research cannot be guessed, but it is a message that will be valid for Christians, Jews, Muslims and all mankind. My personal hope is that it will restore the faith of millions in spiritual values, and unite men in a true awareness of their brotherhood while there is still time.

Selected Bibliography

The Bible was plainly the main source book, but numerous others have provided background information and ideas. The following include those to which I know I am most indebted:

Barbet, P., *A Doctor at Calvary* (trans. the Earl of Wicklow), Clonmore & Reynolds, Dublin, 1954.

Bouquet, A. C., *Life in New Testament Times*, Batsford, London, 1953.

Brandon, S. G. F., *The Trial of Jesus of Nazareth*, Batsford, London, 1968.

Brown, R. E., *Jesus, God and Man*, Chapman, London, 1968.

Bruce, F. F., *New Testament History*, Nelson, London, 1969.

Daniel-Rops, *Jesus in His Time* (trans. R. W. Millar), Eyre & Spottiswoode, London, 1955.

Humber, T., *The Fifth Gospel*, Pocket Books, New York, 1974.

Jeremias, J., *Jerusalem in the Time of Jesus* (trans. F. H. and C. H. Cave), SCM Press, London, 1969.

Jeremias, J., *The Eucharistic Words of Jesus* (trans. N. Perrin), SCM Press, London, 1970.

Marxsen, W., *The Resurrection of Jesus of Nazareth* (trans. M. Kohl), SCM Press, London, 1970.

Morison, F., *Who Moved the Stone?*, Faber & Faber, London, 1930.

Morton, H. V., *In the Steps of the Master*, Methuen, London, 1934.

Reban, J., *Inquest on Jesus Christ* (trans. W. Frischauer), Frewin, London, 1967.

Robinson, J., *The Human Face of God*, SCM Press, London, 1972.

Rinaldi, P. M., *The Man in the Shroud*, Sidgwick & Jackson, London, 1974.

Schonfield, H., *The Passover Plot*, Hutchinson, London, 1965.

Schonfield, H., *The Pentecost Revolution*, Macdonald, London, 1974.

Strauss, D. F., *A New Life of Jesus*, London, 1865.

Walsh, J., *The Shroud*, W. H. Allen, London, 1964.

INDEX